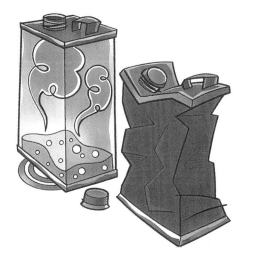

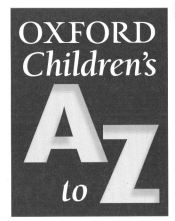

Science

Terry Jennings

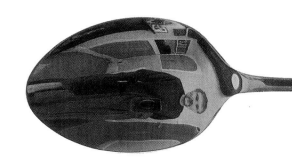

OXFORD
UNIVERSITY PRESS

OXFORD
UNIVERSITY PRESS

Great Clarendon Street, Oxford OX2 6DP

Oxford University Press is a department of the University of Oxford.
It furthers the University's objective of excellence in research, scholarship, and education by publishing worldwide in

Oxford New York

Auckland Bangkok Buenos Aires Cape Town Chennai
Dar es Salaam Delhi Hong Kong Istanbul Karachi Kolkata
Kuala Lumpur Madrid Melbourne Mexico City Mumbai Nairobi
São Paulo Shanghai Taipei Tokyo Toronto

Oxford is a registered trade mark of Oxford University Press
in the UK and in certain other countries

© Terry Jennings 1996
The moral rights of the author have been asserted
Database right Oxford University Press (maker)

This edition 2003

British Library Cataloguing in Publication Data available

ISBN 978-0-19-910992-0

10 9 8 7 6 5 4

Printed in China

Acknowledgements

Design: Designers & Partners

Art Direction: Susan Williams

Picture research: Suzanne Williams

Abbreviations: t = top; b = bottom; l = left; r = right; c = centre; back = background

Photographs

The publishers would like to thank the following for permission to reproduce the following photographs:

Allsport: 23tr/Kurt Ansler/Vandystadt, 28tr/Pascal Rondeau, 33;

Courtesy of The British Petroleum Company p.l.c.: 18;

Magnum Photos/Chris Steele-Perkins: 42t;

Michael Holford: 17c, 23br, 38tr;

OUP Archive/Photo Martin Sookias: 1bl and r, 16, 35c, 35b, 38bl, 42bc, 51, 60-61b;

Oxford Scientific Films/Joaquin Gutierrez Acha: 11;

Science Photo Library: 8b/David Nunuk, 9ct/Alfred Pasieka, 9b/Simon Fraser, 10t/Roger Ressmeyer, 10b/Astrid & Hanns Frieder Michler, 12t/Astrid & Hanns Frieder Michler, 13tl/Claude Nuridsany & Marie Perennou, 13r/Geoff Thompkinson, 14/Tony Craddock, 17r/Roberto de Gugliemo, 21/Peter Menzel, 22 (heading panel) and 23cl/Heini Scneebeli, 22bc/Peter Ryan, 22cr/Los Alamos National Laboratory, 26/Simon Fraser, 28c/Sinclair Stammers, 30/31b/NASA, 31t/Roberto de Gugliemo, 31b/NASA, 37/Adrienne Hart-Davis, 40, 41c/CNRI, 50/Vanessa Vick, 52/Roberto de Gugliemo, 54/John Walsh, 56/Jerry Mason, 59/Claude Nuridsany & Marie Perennou, 61t/Custom Medical Stock Photo, 62, 64/Alexander Tsiaras;

TRIP/W Jacobs: 23tl;

Zefa: 6t, 28l/Boesch, 41tr

Illustrations and diagrams

David Hardy: 43c;

John Haslam: 1tl, 2br, bl, 3tl, cl, bl and r, 4t and b, 5c and b, 10b, 14r, 17t, 18/19c, 19b, 21r, 22/23, 24, 27br, 31b, 32bl, 36, 38/39, 44, 46l, 46/47c, 51cb, 53 border, 54/55cl and b, 56/57c, 58/59b, 60l, 61cr, 62c and b;

Nick Hawken: 1c and tr, 5t, 8, 15b, 26tl, 30c, 33t, 34t, 35c and b, 37c, 47r, 57b, 58/59t;

George Hollingworth: 3cl, 8/9b, 16b and br, 19tl, 20b, 26b, 27cl, 29b, 32/33 border, 42b, 45r, 50/51c, 52c, 52/53c, 56cl, 63br, 64;

Peter Visscher: 2ct, 6/7, 12bl, 15t, 18b, 21t, 25, 29tr, 40/41, 48/49, 55cr

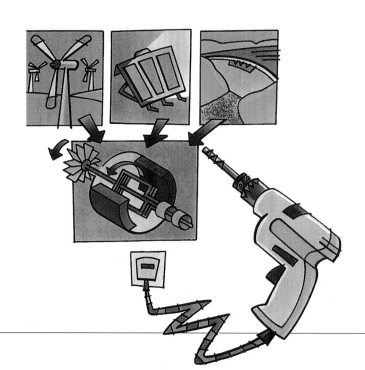

Dear Reader

You hear a reporter on TV talk about **global warming** and you read in a newspaper that **asbestos** is harmful. You can tune in to your local radio station on a certain **frequency**. Do you know what these words mean? Turn the pages of this book and find out about these and another 300 words from science.

What is science? The word science simply means 'knowledge' and scientists gain knowledge by studying the world around us. This book deals with many different kinds of science: chemistry looks at what things like air, water and steel are made up of, and physics explores forms of energy, such as heat, light and sound. Geology studies the Earth and biology investigates plants and animals.

Discover the word for the force that holds us on Earth or the word for an animal that only eats plants. Look further and learn why we see a rainbow in a bubble or how rust forms on iron objects. Enjoy finding out about science and how it plays an important part in your life.

Terry Jennings

A

absorb

To absorb means to soak something up. A sponge or dry cloth will absorb spilt water. The roots of a plant absorb water from the soil. Green leaves absorb sunlight to make food. In humans and other animals, the blood absorbs **oxygen** from the lungs.

acid

An acid is a **chemical** that will **neutralize** a **base** such as an **alkali**. There are many different kinds of acid. Lemons are sour because they contain citric acid. The acid in vinegar is called acetic acid, and that in the sting of some ants is called formic acid.

Strong acids are dangerous and have to be handled very carefully. They can dissolve metals and clothes, and can burn skin.

Acids have many uses. Weak acids, such as vinegar, are used to 'pickle' foods to preserve them. Car batteries contain a strong acid called sulphuric acid. Acids are used to make many other chemicals and materials, including dyes, detergents and plastics.
See also **alkali**, **pH**.

acid rain

Acid rain is a kind of **pollution**. It is caused by certain **gases** which come from the chimneys of factories and power stations and from the engines of cars and other motor vehicles. The gases **dissolve** in rain, hail or snow and form an **acid** that may be as strong as lemon juice or vinegar. There is a little bit of acid in all rain but acid rain causes damage as it contains more acid.

pressure
aerosol spray
button
nozzle
liquid which turns to spray
aerosol can

aerosol

An aerosol is a fine mist or spray. Many substances can be sprayed as an aerosol. These include paint, polishes, deodorants, fly killers and oven cleaners. A can holds the substance under **pressure**, so when you press a button on the can the aerosol is sprayed. The can may also be called an aerosol.

In recent years scientists have become worried that some of the liquids or gases that help an aerosol can to spray may be polluting our world. Aerosol cans that do not cause this **pollution** often have 'Ozone Friendly' printed on them. See also **ozone**.

Acid rain kills many water plants and animals. It makes trees lose their leaves and eats away the stonework of buildings.

waste gases mix with water in clouds

acids are formed

waste gases

acids fall as acid rain

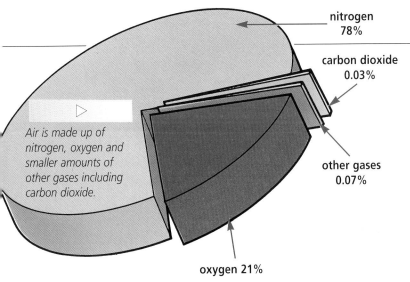

nitrogen 78%

carbon dioxide 0.03%

other gases 0.07%

oxygen 21%

Air is made up of nitrogen, oxygen and smaller amounts of other gases including carbon dioxide.

air

Air is the mixture of gases that makes up the Earth's **atmosphere**. Air also contains some water vapour, as well as dust and other kinds of **pollution**.

We cannot see air, nor can we smell or taste it. We can, however, feel the air when the wind blows. All living things need oxygen from the air for **respiration**. Many animals get this oxygen by **breathing**.

alcohol

Alcohol is a liquid that burns easily and evaporates very quickly. Most people have heard of the alcohol called ethanol that is found in such drinks as beer, wine and whisky. Drinking too much of this alcohol stops people thinking or seeing clearly, and it can be harmful to other parts of the body, like the liver.

There are many other kinds of alcohol. They are used in **antifreeze**, paints, glues, aftershaves, printing inks and dry-cleaning liquids. This is because alcohols dissolve many things that will not dissolve in water.

Many household items are made with aluminium.

alkali

An alkali is the chemical opposite of an **acid**. It is a **chemical** that when mixed with an acid can **neutralize**, or cancel out, the acid effect. Strong alkalis, like strong acids, can burn the skin or clothing.

Alkalis are used to make soaps, dyes, glass and household cleaners. Toothpaste contains alkalis to neutralize the acid in the mouth which makes teeth decay. Indigestion mixtures contain alkalis to neutralize the acid in the stomach. Lime, which is spread on the soil to make it less acid, is also an alkali.
See also **acid, base, pH**.

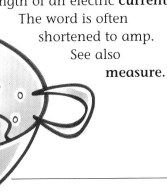

alloy

An alloy is a **metal** which is made by melting and mixing together two or more other metals. Brass is an alloy made from copper and zinc. Bronze, used for statues, ornaments and church bells, is an alloy of tin and copper.

aluminium

Aluminium is a silvery-white **metal**. It is softer and lighter than most metals such as iron or steel, and it does not rust or corrode.

Because it is such a light **element**, aluminium is used in making aircraft, saucepans, electric cables and thin sheets of foil wrapped around chocolate bars. Many drinks cans are also made from aluminium. Most aluminium is obtained from a type of rock called bauxite.

ampere

An ampere is the unit used in measuring the strength of an electric **current**. The word is often shortened to amp. See also **measure**.

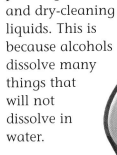

Animals

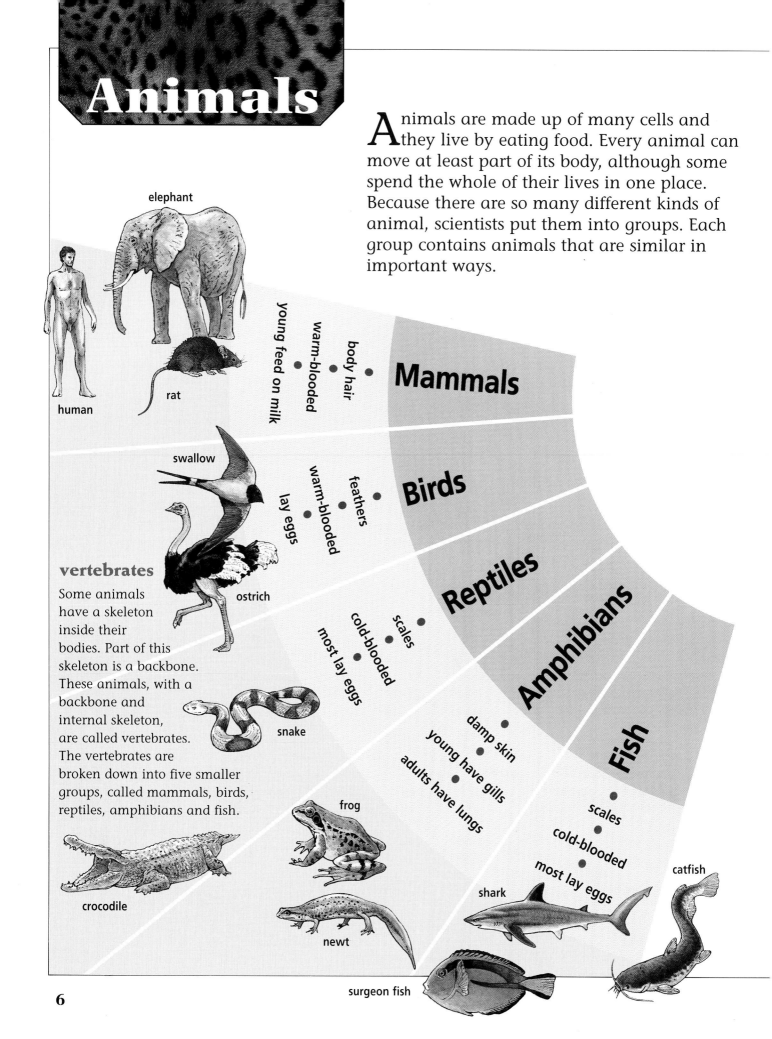

Animals are made up of many cells and they live by eating food. Every animal can move at least part of its body, although some spend the whole of their lives in one place. Because there are so many different kinds of animal, scientists put them into groups. Each group contains animals that are similar in important ways.

elephant

human

rat

Mammals

young feed on milk

warm-blooded

body hair

swallow

ostrich

Birds

lay eggs

warm-blooded

feathers

vertebrates

Some animals have a skeleton inside their bodies. Part of this skeleton is a backbone. These animals, with a backbone and internal skeleton, are called vertebrates. The vertebrates are broken down into five smaller groups, called mammals, birds, reptiles, amphibians and fish.

snake

Reptiles

scales

cold-blooded

most lay eggs

Amphibians

damp skin

young have gills

adults have lungs

crocodile

frog

newt

Fish

scales

cold-blooded

most lay eggs

shark

catfish

surgeon fish

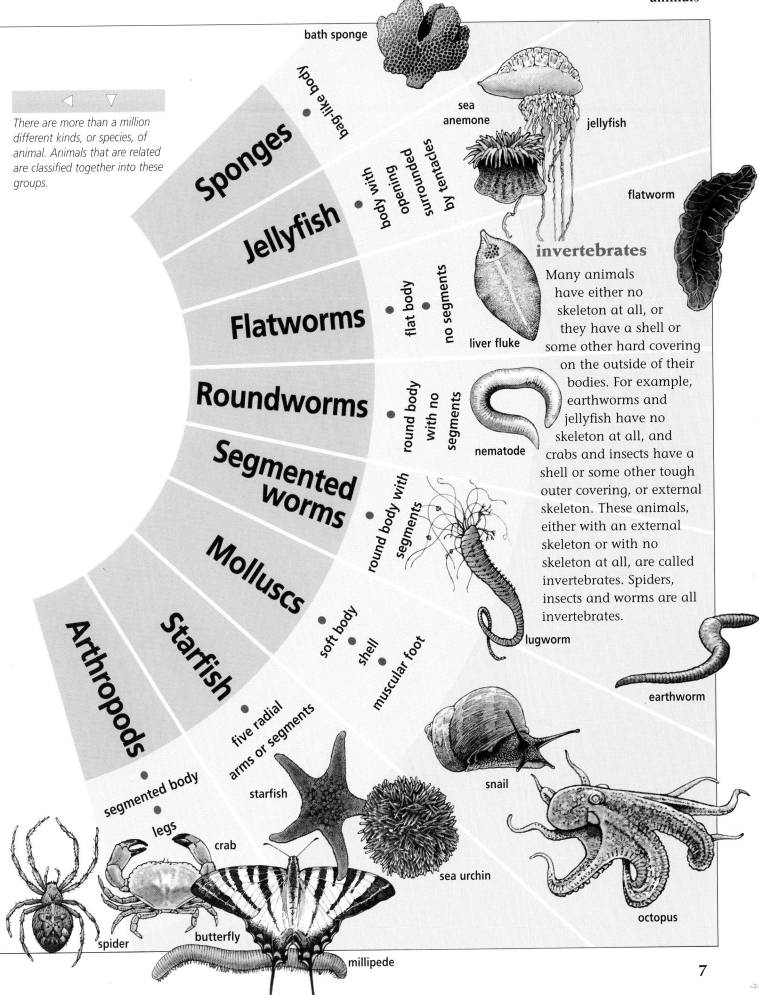

There are more than a million different kinds, or species, of animal. Animals that are related are classified together into these groups.

bath sponge

Sponges

bag-like body

sea anemone

jellyfish

Jellyfish

body with opening surrounded by tentacles

flatworm

Flatworms

flat body

no segments

liver fluke

invertebrates

Many animals have either no skeleton at all, or they have a shell or some other hard covering on the outside of their bodies. For example, earthworms and jellyfish have no skeleton at all, and crabs and insects have a shell or some other tough outer covering, or external skeleton. These animals, either with an external skeleton or with no skeleton at all, are called invertebrates. Spiders, insects and worms are all invertebrates.

Roundworms

round body with no segments

nematode

Segmented worms

round body with segments

lugworm

earthworm

Molluscs

soft body

shell

muscular foot

Starfish

five radial arms or segments

snail

Arthropods

segmented body

legs

starfish

crab

sea urchin

octopus

spider

butterfly

millipede

antifreeze

An antifreeze is a liquid added to water to stop it freezing. The antifreeze used most often is an **alcohol** called ethylene glycol. It is put in the radiators of cars to stop the cooling water from freezing in cold weather and damaging the engine. This is because antifreeze lowers the temperature at which water freezes.

asbestos

Asbestos is a greyish-white **mineral**. It is made up of **fibres** which do not burn, and these fibres can be woven into the fireproof clothing worn by firefighters.

Asbestos is also used to make parts of the brakes and clutches of motor vehicles. These get very hot because they rub against other parts. As asbestos can be very harmful to people, it has to be used with great care.

astronomy

Astronomy is finding out about the **Sun**, **Moon**, **stars**, **planets** and other objects in **space**. The scientists who study these objects are called astronomers. They work in special buildings known as observatories. They use telescopes, satellites, computers and many other instruments in their work.

▽ The domes on the outside of this observatory house the large telescopes inside.

▷ This diagram shows the layers of the atmosphere.

atmosphere

The atmosphere is the thick layer of **air** that surrounds the **Earth**. The atmosphere is about 500 kilometres deep and is made up of four layers. The layer where we live, and where our weather is formed, is called the troposphere. The other layers are the stratosphere, the ionosphere and the exosphere.

The air which makes up our atmosphere is a mixture of **gases**, mainly **nitrogen** and **oxygen**. The other planets, such as Mars and Venus, have atmospheres made up of different gases.

exosphere

ionosphere

stratosphere

troposphere

atom

An atom is the tiniest part of something that cannot easily be split into something smaller. Everything in the world and in space is made up of atoms. There are many different atoms, although each of the chemical **elements** is made up of one type of atom only. Each atom itself is made up of tiny **particles**. Although all atoms are roughly the same size, they do not all have the same number of particles in them. See also **molecule**.

▷ A model showing the particles that make up a helium atom. Atoms are so small that 9 million million could cover one of the full stops on this page.

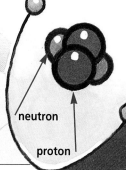

electron

neutron

proton

bacteria

Bacteria are tiny living things. Some bacteria are harmful **germs** that cause disease. Other bacteria are useful and break down dead plants and animals, returning them as plant foods to the soil.
See also **virus**.

▷
In warm, moist places bacteria breed very quickly. One bacterium can divide in two in 20 minutes. In 24 hours there would be about 4000 million million million bacteria.

balance

A balance is an instrument used to measure the **weight** or **mass** of something.

base

A base is a **chemical** substance that will **neutralize** an **acid**. **Alkalis** are examples of bases.
See also **pH**.

battery

A battery makes and stores **electricity**. Small electric batteries are used to run torches, radios, calculators and watches. Large electric batteries are used to start car engines and even to drive electric vehicles and some small cars.

Small batteries are usually of a kind called simple **cells**. The electricity comes from **chemicals** sealed inside them. Once the battery is 'flat' it can produce no more electricity and is then usually thrown away.

Large batteries also use chemicals to make electricity. But when the chemicals begin to run out, they can be renewed. To do this, electricity is fed into the battery. This is called recharging.

biodegradable

A biodegradable material is one that can rot away after we have used it. Materials made from plants and animals are biodegradable. They usually rot and **decay** away quickly as a result of the action of **microbes**.

Many **synthetic** materials, including most **plastics**, are not biodegradable. Plastic wrappers and other plastic litter cause **pollution**.

biology

Biology is finding out about plants, animals and other living things. Biologists are scientists who study what plants and animals look like, and how they live and grow.

◁
Plastic litter that is not biodegradable may still be around in hundreds of years' time.

In this biotechnological experiment air, food and water are used and reused by bacteria.

biotechnology

Biotechnology is the way people use **bacteria** and fungi to make useful materials. For hundreds of years people have used the tiny fungus yeast to help make wine, beer and bread. When some bacteria feed on household waste, they produce a **gas** called methane. This is used as a **fuel**. Some other bacteria help turn milk into cheese or yoghurt.

boiling

Boiling is what happens when a **liquid** changes into a **gas**. When a liquid such as water is heated, the tiny particles it is made of move faster and faster. Eventually they break free and the liquid boils.

When water is heated, the gas called water vapour is produced. Water boils at 100°C (degrees Celsius) at sea level. If you climb a high mountain though, where the air **pressure** is less, the water will boil at a much lower **temperature**.
See also **freeze, water, vapour**.

bond

A bond is a strong force holding two **atoms** together in a **molecule** or **compound**.

botany

Botany is finding out about **plants**. People have always studied plants, because from them we get food, fuel, medicines and materials for clothes and building. Botanists are scientists who study the many different kinds of plants.

breathing

Breathing is what animals do when they take air into their lungs and give it out again. All animals need **oxygen** from the air so that they can burn up **food** to produce **energy** in their bodies. This is called **respiration**. Breathing takes air into the body so that oxygen can be absorbed by the blood.

bulb

A bulb, or electric light bulb, is used for producing **light**. It has a very thin wire, called a filament, in it. When an electric **current** passes through the filament, it glows white hot and gives off light. A special **gas** inside the bulb stops the filament from burning away too quickly.

burning

Burning is what happens when something combines very rapidly with **oxygen** in the air, to give **light** and **heat**. The heat and light form **fire**.

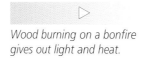

Wood burning on a bonfire gives out light and heat.

A tree frog is camouflaged amongst the leaves it lives in.

camouflage

Camouflage is the way some animals protect themselves from their enemies. Many animals have colours, patterns and shapes which make them hard to see.

carbohydrate

A carbohydrate, which is a substance found in living things, is made up of only **carbon**, **hydrogen**, and **oxygen**. Starch, sugar and cellulose are carbohydrates.

All carbohydrates, including sugars and starches, are made by green plants. These are an important part of the **food** of humans and other animals as they provide energy. Animals get the carbohydrates they need by eating plants, or other animals which have eaten plants, or sometimes both.
See also **food chain**.

carbon

Carbon is one of the main chemical **elements** found in the bodies of living things. Human beings are 20 per cent carbon, while grass is about 4 per cent carbon.

Carbon is also found in non-living things such as **coal**, **oil**, **natural gas**, peat and wood. **Diamonds** are crystals of carbon. Graphite (pencil 'lead'), **charcoal** and soot are also forms of carbon.

All the carbon in the world is used over and over again, in what is called the carbon cycle.

carbon dioxide

Carbon dioxide is one of the **gases** in the **air**. It is made up of the elements **carbon** and **oxygen** and has no colour or smell. The air breathed out by animals contains more carbon dioxide than the same air when it was breathed in. Plants use carbon dioxide from the air to make their own food by **photosynthesis**. When any substance containing carbon burns, carbon dioxide is given off. It is one of the gases which absorb heat and trap it near the Earth's surface, causing the **greenhouse effect**.

carnivore

A carnivore is an **animal** which eats mainly flesh. Lions, tigers, bears, dogs, cats and eagles are carnivores. Their bodies are specially suited to catching prey and biting and digesting the flesh. A few plants, such as the sundew and Venus flytrap, catch insects. They are called carnivorous plants.
See also **herbivore**, **omnivore**.

carbon dioxide in air

photosynthesis

burning fuels

respiration

microbes in the ground

fossil fuels

catalyst

A catalyst is a **chemical** that changes the speed of a **reaction** without itself being changed. It may make a reaction faster or it may slow it down. Catalysts are used in industry to increase the production of **materials**. **Enzymes** are natural catalysts that speed up reactions in animals and plants.

An ammonite fossilized in chalk nearly 200 million years ago.

cell

A cell is a tiny part of a living thing. A single cell can be a complete **organism**, such as an amoeba or bacterium, or just one of many cells that make up a plant or animal. There are many different kinds of cell and each kind has a special job to do. The largest cell in the human body is the **egg** cell produced by a woman. It is about the size of one of the full stops on this page.

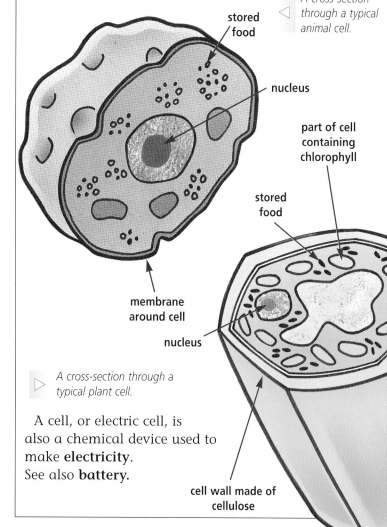

A cross-section through a typical animal cell.

stored food

nucleus

membrane around cell

part of cell containing chlorophyll

stored food

nucleus

A cross-section through a typical plant cell.

A cell, or electric cell, is also a chemical device used to make **electricity**.
See also **battery**.

cell wall made of cellulose

chalk

Chalk is a soft, greyish-white rock. It is a rock that is made of tiny **fossil** seashells. Water can soak through chalk quite easily.

Chalk is a special kind of limestone. Limestone itself is formed from the remains of tiny living things and rocks that have gradually been broken down into sand, silt and mud. These settle at the bottom of lakes and seas and slowly harden into limestone. From limestone, lime is made. Limestone is also used to make cement and in making **iron**.

charcoal

Charcoal is a black or very dark grey substance which is mainly **carbon**. You have probably seen it used as a **fuel** in barbecues. Charcoal is made when wood is partly burnt in a special oven where there is little or no air. Charcoal has been used as a fuel since early times. Scientists use charcoal to **absorb** gases and liquids, while artists use charcoal pencils.

charge

Charge, or electric charge, is an amount of **electricity** held in something. Charge can be either positive or negative.
See also **current**.

chemical

A chemical is a pure **element**, or any **substance** formed when two or more elements join together to form a **compound**. All substances are chemicals or mixtures of chemicals. Metals, plastics, air, water and human beings are made from chemicals. Some chemicals, such as iron and carbon, are **solids** and some, such as water and sulphuric acid, are **liquids**. Other chemicals, such as hydrogen, oxygen and carbon dioxide, are **gases**.

About 4 million different chemicals have been discovered, and more than 5000 new ones are discovered every week.

Crystals of the pure chemical element iodine give off a violet vapour when heated.

Some chemicals are made by humans and some occur naturally. They have many uses. Many are medicines, some kill germs, while others stop food going bad. Some chemicals, called fertilizers, help plants to grow better, while other chemicals kill insect pests. Materials such as metals and plastics are made using chemicals.

Paper chromatography is used to test the purity of chemicals.

chemistry

Chemistry is the study of **chemicals** and the **elements**. A person who studies chemicals and the elements is called a chemist. Chemists find out what atoms are in chemicals, how they are affected by heat and pressure, what special properties they have, and how **reactions** between them take place.

chlorophyll

Chlorophyll is the pigment that gives **plants** their green colour. Chlorophyll helps a plant to make its own **food** by using sunlight. The light energy is trapped by chlorophyll and used to turn **carbon dioxide** and water into sugar and oxygen. This process is called **photosynthesis**. Most plant cells do not make chlorophyll unless they are in the light.

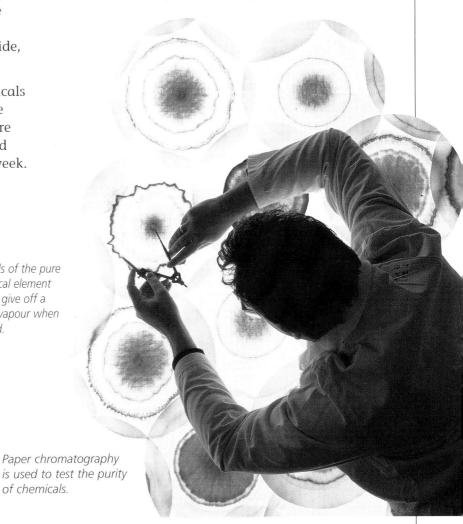

chromatography

Chromatography is a way of separating mixtures of substances to see what they are made of. It is used to separate mixtures of **liquids** or **gases**.

If a coloured chocolate drop is shaken with a little water, a coloured solution is formed. If a drop or two of this is placed on filter paper, some of the substances are soaked up faster than others. They separate as rings of different colours. This is a form of paper chromatography.

chromosome

Chromosomes are found inside the nucleus of a **cell**. They are made from the molecule **DNA** and can only be seen with a microscope. Chromosomes occur in pairs and can be seen most easily when a cell is dividing. Each kind of plant or animal has its own particular number of chromosomes.

Chromosomes carry the plans, or **genes**, of a plant or animal. The genes hold information such as the type and characteristics of the animal or plant. When plants and animals **reproduce**, chromosomes and genes from both parents are mixed together.

nucleus

chromosome

cell

▷ *Coils of DNA make up the thread-like chromosomes of a cell.*

coiled DNA molecule

classification

Classification is the ordering of **organisms**, such as plants and animals, into groups. Each group contains organisms that are similar in important ways.
See also **kingdom, species.**

clay

Clay is a kind of sticky rock. It is made up of very fine particles, or grains. Water drains through clay very slowly. Clay is used in making bricks and pottery.

coal

Coal is a hard, black **mineral**. It consists mostly of the element **carbon** and was formed millions of years ago from the rotting remains of trees and other plants growing in tropical forests. This rotting plant material gradually became covered by rocks and slowly turned to coal. Most coal is found in bands or seams under the ground from which it is mined and used as a **fuel**.

Coal is called a **fossil fuel** because it comes from the remains of very old plants. Along with **oil**, it is one of the main fossil fuels in the world.

◁ *This excavator is being used in an open-cast coal mine.*

circuit

A circuit is the path an electric **current** takes round a loop of wires and connections. If there is a break in a circuit, the electric current will not flow.

A circuit-breaker is a safety device that stops the flow of current in an electric circuit if a fault occurs and the current becomes dangerously high.

cold-blooded

A cold-blooded animal is one that cannot control the **temperature** of its body. The body temperature of these animals changes with that of the air or water around them. When it is warm, the animal's body and blood are warm. When it is cold, the animal's body and blood are cold and it cannot be active.
See also **warm-blooded.**

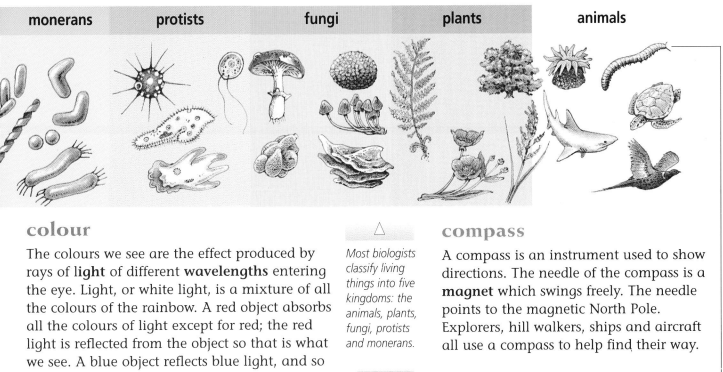

colour

The colours we see are the effect produced by rays of **light** of different **wavelengths** entering the eye. Light, or white light, is a mixture of all the colours of the rainbow. A red object absorbs all the colours of light except for red; the red light is reflected from the object so that is what we see. A blue object reflects blue light, and so on.

There are some special colours which can be mixed together to make any other colour. These are called primary colours. The primary colours of paint are red, yellow and blue. When mixed together in equal amounts, these three colours make black. The primary colours of light are red, green and blue. A mixture of these three colours produces white. See also **light**, **radiation**.

Most biologists classify living things into five kingdoms: the animals, plants, fungi, protists and monerans.

A bubble acts as a prism, splitting light into all its colours.

combustion

Combustion is another word for catching fire and **burning**.

compass

A compass is an instrument used to show directions. The needle of the compass is a **magnet** which swings freely. The needle points to the magnetic North Pole. Explorers, hill walkers, ships and aircraft all use a compass to help find their way.

compound

A compound is a **chemical** made from two or more **elements** joined together in fixed amounts. The **atoms** of the elements in a compound are joined by chemical **bonds**.

compress

To compress a substance is to squeeze it by a **force** so that it takes up less space.

White light is not a single colour but a mixture of all the colours of the rainbow.

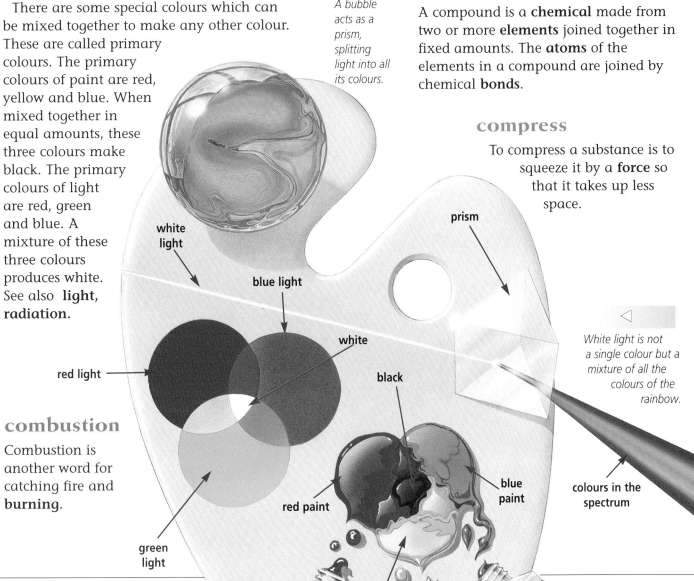

white light

blue light

white

red light

black

prism

green light

red paint

yellow paint

blue paint

colours in the spectrum

condense

To condense is to become squeezed into a smaller space. A **vapour** or **gas** condenses to form a **liquid** when it cools. A liquid takes up less space than a gas. Some of the water vapour in the air in a warm kitchen often condenses as water droplets on the windows. Mist, fog and clouds are produced when the water vapour in moist air condenses into very small droplets. If the droplets are large enough, they fall as rain.

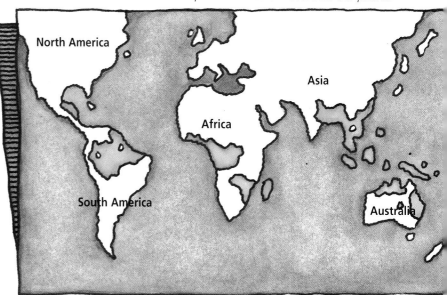

Children playing a game with condensation on a window.

conductor

A conductor is a material which transmits certain kinds of **energy**, such as **hea**t and **electricity**. Metals are the best conductors of heat or electricity. This is because their **electrons** can move freely, carrying the electric **current** or heat with them. A semi-conductor is a material, such as **silicon**, that conducts heat or electricity but not as well as a conductor.

Conduction describes the way which heat, electricity and other types of energy flow through a solid object.
See also **insulate**.

conservation

Conservation is the protection and careful use of forests, rivers, seas, countryside, soils and other parts of your natural surroundings. Conservation is also the protection of animals and plants in their natural surroundings. Another meaning of conservation is the careful use of natural products, such as coal, oil and wood.

▽ *Rainforests (shown in green) make up one third of the land area on Earth. They need to be conserved in order to keep the balance of nature on our planet.*

▷ *The metal spoon becomes too hot to hold as it conducts heat from the hot drink.*

North America

Asia

Africa

South America

Australia

contract

To contract is to become shorter or smaller in size. Most **solids**, **liquids** and **gases** contract when they are cooled.

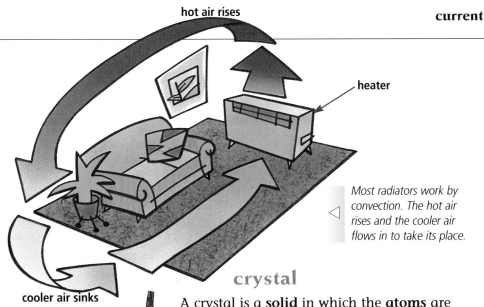

Most radiators work by convection. The hot air rises and the cooler air flows in to take its place.

heater

cooler air sinks

convection

Convection is a way in which **heat** flows through a **liquid** or a **gas**. When a liquid or gas is heated, the hot part **expands** and becomes less dense. The hot liquid or gas rises and cooler liquid or gas flows into its place. In this way the heat is spread.

copper

Copper is a soft, reddish-brown **metal**. It is a good conductor of **heat** and **electricity** and is easily bent and shaped or drawn out into wires. It is used for making electrical cables and for water pipes. Copper is an **element** that is used to make **alloys** such as brass and bronze. Most 'copper' coins are in fact made of copper alloys.

corrosion

Corrosion is the slow change on the surface of a **metal** by **chemicals** in the air. The corrosion of iron by moist air produces **rust**. Air **pollution** by gases, such as sulphur dioxide and nitrogen dioxide, which produce **acid rain**, makes metals corrode quickly. Painting or coating metal helps to stop it corroding. Steel bicycle parts and bathroom taps are often coated with a thin layer of chromium. Cutlery may be coated with silver, nickel or chromium to stop or reduce corrosion.

▷

This sword is more than 900 years old. The iron blade has corroded yet the gold and silver hilt has not been changed by moist air.

crystal

A crystal is a **solid** in which the **atoms** are arranged in regular patterns like bathroom tiles. Crystals often have a definite shape with straight edges and flat faces.

Most solids can form crystals, including rocks, minerals, metals, plastics and everyday substances such as salt and sugar. Crystals usually form when molten rocks or other molten solids cool down and harden. Crystals also form when a solution of a substance is allowed to **evaporate** slowly, or when a strong or saturated solution of a substance cools.

▷

The straight edges and flat faces are clearly seen on these crystals.

current

A current, or electric current, is a flow of **electrons**, or negative electric **charge**. If electrons move from one **atom** to another, they flow as an electric current. Electric currents are caused by **energy** pushing electrons round a circuit. The energy may be provided by a **battery** or mains electricity. Electric current is measured in **amperes**.
See also **electricity, measure**.

D

decay

Decay is what happens when dead plants and animals rot away. It is caused by **bacteria** and fungi in the soil.

Radioactive substances are also said to decay when they slowly break down into smaller substances.

decompose

Chemists use the word decompose to describe what happens when a chemical substance breaks down into simpler substances.

The remains of dead plants and animals decompose in the soil. A decomposer is a living thing which causes dead plants and animals to rot or decompose away. **Bacteria** and fungi are decomposers.

degree

The **temperature** of something is measured in degrees. A degree is a unit of temperature.
See also **measure**.

density

Density is a measure of how heavy something is for its size. It is measured by dividing the **mass** of an object by its **volume**. A model ship made of lead is much heavier for its size, or denser, than the same model ship made of wood.

Diamonds are used on the machines that are used to drill for oil.

detergent

A detergent is a chemical substance used to remove dirt, oil or grease. Detergents can be liquids, as in shampoos and washing-up liquids, or powdered solids. Detergents are made from **oil**.

diamond

Diamond is a very hard gemstone. It is the hardest known substance found in nature and is used in cutting tools, including dentists' drills, and as a precious stone. Diamond is a special form of the element **carbon**. The **atoms** of carbon are arranged so regularly that they form **crystals**.

Diamonds were formed millions of years ago in volcanic rocks at extremely high pressures and temperatures. The largest diamond ever found weighed 621 grams. It was found in South Africa in 1905.

digestion

Digestion is what animals, and a few plants, do to their **food**. Digestion breaks down the food into simpler substances. The animal or plant can then use these substances to help it **grow** and to produce **energy**. Waste material in the food is not used and it passes out of the body.
See also **fibre**.

Liquids can be purified by distilling them.

Densities of different materials measured in kilograms per cubic metre (kg/m³).

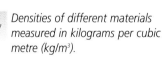

wood
(750 kg/m³)

petrol
(800 kg/m³)

water
(1000 kg/m³)

aluminium
(2700 kg/m³)

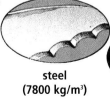

steel
(7800 kg/m³)

lead
(11 300 kg/m³)

gold
(19 300 kg/m³)

disease

solid

A disease is a sickness, or illness, of a plant or animal. A disease stops the plant or animal from working properly. Some diseases are caused by **bacteria** and **viruses**, some by lack of certain **foods** and a few by fungi. Some human diseases, such as the common cold, can be very mild; others, like cancer, are very serious.

solid dissolves in liquid

dissolve

When a **solid** substance or a **gas** is taken into water or some other liquid, then it dissolves in the liquid. The solid or gas and the liquid it dissolves in form a **solution**. Sugar dissolves in water and makes a sugar solution. The sugar is said to be soluble in the water.

solution

distil

To distil a liquid is to **purify** it. This is done by boiling the liquid and then cooling some or all of the vapour back into a pure liquid. Distillation is also used to separate a mixture of liquids with different boiling points. See also **condense**.

DNA

DNA is a short way of writing deoxyribonucleic acid. This is a large molecule found in the **nucleus** of nearly every living **cell**. DNA makes up **chromosomes** which carry **genes**. All the information that a living thing inherits from its parents is stored in DNA. There are nearly 6 billion people in the world and, apart from identical twins, they all have different DNA. If one cell was taken from each of them, and all the DNA removed, it would weigh only 0.025 grams.

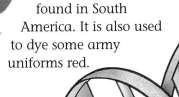

You distil a liquid by boiling it and then cooling the vapour.

drug

A drug is a substance used as a medicine to kill pain or cure a **disease**.

Other kinds of drugs can harm your mind or your senses. Heroin is a harmful drug.

dry ice

Dry ice is frozen **carbon dioxide**. It is extremely cold and scientists use it to cool things down. If warm air is blown over dry ice, then it changes to a dense white cloud. This effect is sometimes used in the theatre.

dye

A dye is a substance used to give **colour** to hair, cloth, leather, paper, plastics and some foods. Some dyes are natural **chemicals** taken from plants and animals, but most are made from chemicals in a **laboratory**. The red dye used in certain foods is obtained from the cochineal beetle found in South America. It is also used to dye some army uniforms red.

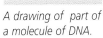

A drawing of part of a molecule of DNA.

Earth

The Earth is the **planet** we live on. It is roughly the shape of a ball. We call this shape a sphere. On the surface of the Earth there is more water than land. Nearly three-quarters of the Earth is covered by oceans and seas.

The Earth was formed about 4600 million years ago. It is believed that it came from a huge cloud of dust and gases swirling in space. Somehow the dust and gases were drawn together and formed a huge ball which glowed red hot. Later the surface of this ball cooled and hardened. Steam rose from the hot ball and formed clouds. As the air around the ball cooled, the clouds cooled and produced rain. It rained for thousands of years. The water filled the hollows on the surface of the ball, our planet Earth, and formed the oceans and seas.

atmosphere

crust

mantle

outer core

inner core

△ The planet as we know it today.

earthquake

An earthquake is a sudden violent shaking of the ground. In a really large earthquake, huge cracks may appear in the ground and buildings may collapse. An earthquake is caused by movements of the Earth's surface, or crust.

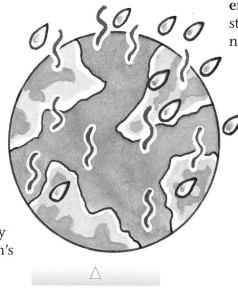

△ Steam from the hot ball formed clouds which then produced rain.

echo

An echo is a **sound** that is heard again as it is bounced off, or reflected from, a hard surface. A special instrument called an echo sounder is used on ships to test the depth of water, using sound. Short bursts of sound are sent down to the seabed. They are bounced off the bottom and collected by the instrument. The depth of the water can be worked out from the time it takes for the echo to return to the sounder. Bats and some sea animals use echoes to find food and to find their way in the dark.

eclipse

A solar eclipse happens when the **Moon** comes between the **Earth** and the **Sun**, so that all or part of the Sun is hidden.

A lunar eclipse happens when the Earth moves between the Sun and the Moon, so that all or part of the Moon is in shadow.

ecology

Ecology is the study of the way in which **animals** and **plants** depend upon each other and upon their natural surroundings, or **environment**. An ecologist is a scientist who studies how animals and plants live in their natural surroundings.

▽ The dust cloud condensed into a hot ball.

▽ The Earth began as a d cloud million: of years ago.

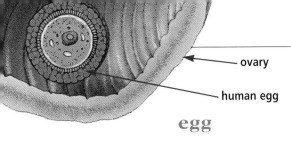

ovary

human egg

A human egg (above) and a fertilized bird's egg (below).

air sac

shell

yolk

egg

An egg is a tiny **cell** which is made by female animals and plants. When it is fertilized by a male cell, an egg can grow into a new animal or plant.

Almost all animals have eggs and most lay them in the outside world. These eggs all contain food in the yolk which allows the young animal to grow. Some eggs are covered in a hard outer shell. We humans, and animals such as dogs, cats, mice and cows (all mammals), do not lay eggs. Instead the egg is fertilized and develops inside the mother's body.
See also **fertilization**.

electricity

Electricity is one kind of **energy**. It is used for lighting, heating, making sound or making machines work. Electricity consists of large numbers of tiny particles, called **electrons**.

Electrons are parts of **atoms**, and since everything is made of atoms, there is electricity in everything. However, you do not notice this electricity until something makes electrons move from their atoms. Rubbing something makes electrons in it move from one atom to another. This is called **static electricity**. If electrons move through wires made of copper and other metals (a **circuit**), then this makes an electric **current**. Batteries or mains electricity push electrons through circuits.
See also **battery, generator**.

A plasma ball is designed to produce static electricity that you can see clearly as it flashes from the centre to the outside of the ball.

electromagnetic radiation

Radio waves, ultraviolet waves, **X-rays**, **microwaves**, **light**, gamma rays and infrared rays are all forms of electromagnetic **radiation**. The waves are made up of electric and magnetic forces.

electron

An electron is a tiny particle that is in orbit around the nucleus of an **atom**.
See also **electricity**.

electronics

Electronics is the study of **electrons** and their uses in science and industry. We use things designed or made by electronic scientists or electronic engineers every day. Radios, TVs, compact disc players, video recorders, computers, calculators, digital watches, X-ray machines and hearing aids all use electronics. Electronics uses tiny electric **currents** flowing through tiny **circuits**.

All these items use electronics to work.

Element

An element is any substance that cannot be broken down into simpler substances. **Carbon dioxide** gas, for example, is made up of **carbon** and **oxygen**, so it is not an element. However, carbon and oxygen cannot be split into anything simpler, so they are elements. Some elements are **solids**, some are **liquids**, some are **gases** at normal temperatures.

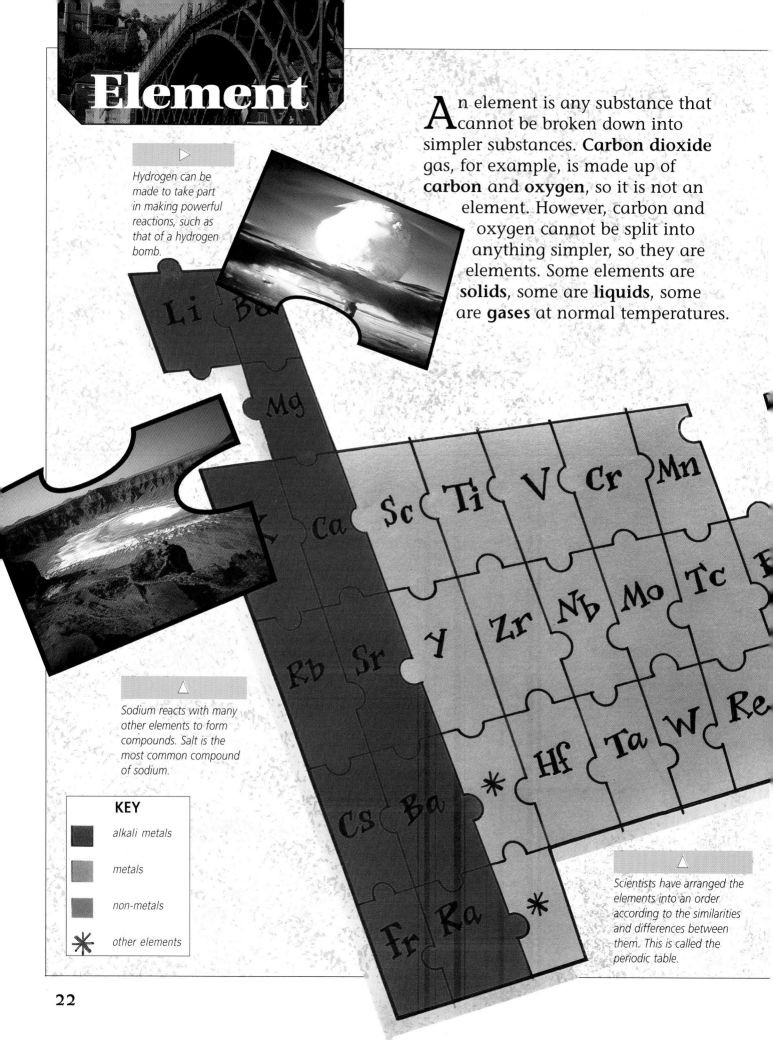

▷
Hydrogen can be made to take part in making powerful reactions, such as that of a hydrogen bomb.

△
Sodium reacts with many other elements to form compounds. Salt is the most common compound of sodium.

KEY

■ alkali metals

■ metals

■ non-metals

✳ other elements

△
Scientists have arranged the elements into an order according to the similarities and differences between them. This is called the periodic table.

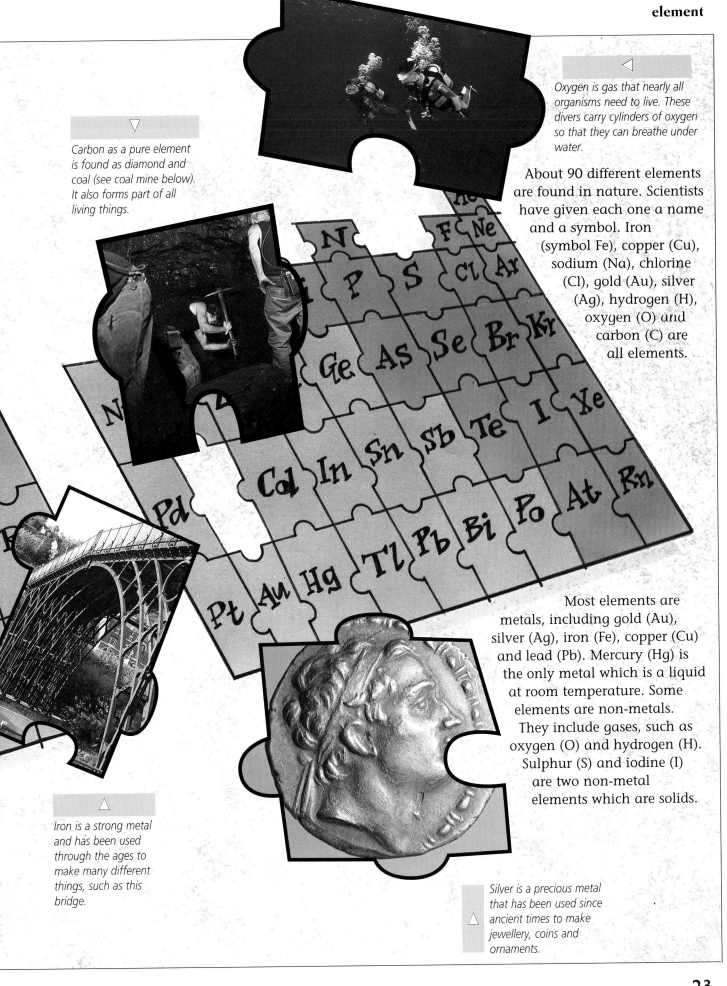

Oxygen is gas that nearly all organisms need to live. These divers carry cylinders of oxygen so that they can breathe under water.

Carbon as a pure element is found as diamond and coal (see coal mine below). It also forms part of all living things.

About 90 different elements are found in nature. Scientists have given each one a name and a symbol. Iron (symbol Fe), copper (Cu), sodium (Na), chlorine (Cl), gold (Au), silver (Ag), hydrogen (H), oxygen (O) and carbon (C) are all elements.

Most elements are metals, including gold (Au), silver (Ag), iron (Fe), copper (Cu) and lead (Pb). Mercury (Hg) is the only metal which is a liquid at room temperature. Some elements are non-metals. They include gases, such as oxygen (O) and hydrogen (H). Sulphur (S) and iodine (I) are two non-metal elements which are solids.

Iron is a strong metal and has been used through the ages to make many different things, such as this bridge.

Silver is a precious metal that has been used since ancient times to make jewellery, coins and ornaments.

energy

Every time you do something you use energy. Energy has been changed from one form to another. Playing games, cooking food and making things all need energy. Nothing can live, work, grow or move without energy.

There are many different kinds of energy. **Light**, **heat**, **sound** and **electricity** are all kinds of energy. **Fuels** and **food** contain chemical energy. The chemical energy stored in fuels can be changed by machines into mechanical energy. Reactions of the nuclei of atoms give another kind of energy called nuclear energy.

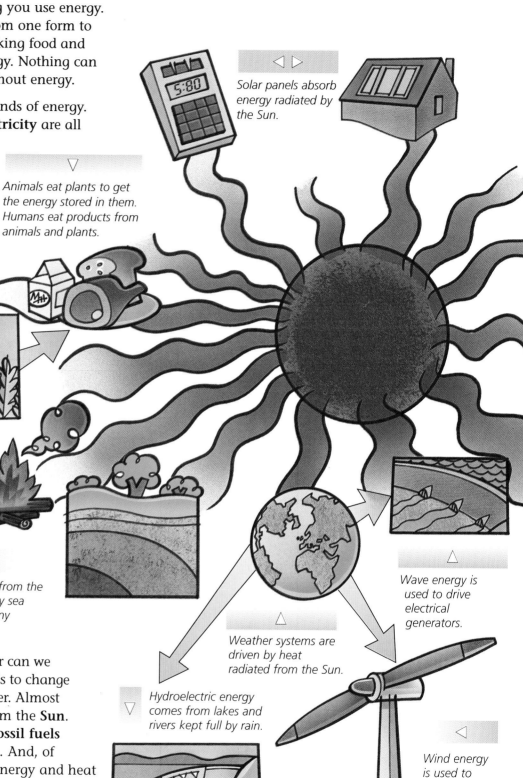

Solar panels absorb energy radiated by the Sun.

Animals eat plants to get the energy stored in them. Humans eat products from animals and plants.

Plants take energy from the Sun to grow.

Wood releases energy when it is burned.

Fossil fuels were formed from the remains of plants and tiny sea creatures which lived many millions of years ago.

Wave energy is used to drive electrical generators.

Weather systems are driven by heat radiated from the Sun.

Hydroelectric energy comes from lakes and rivers kept full by rain.

Wind energy is used to drive electrical generators.

We cannot make energy, nor can we destroy energy. All we can do is to change one kind of energy into another. Almost all of the energy we use is from the **Sun**. The energy in our food and **fossil fuels** came originally from the Sun. And, of course, we also receive light energy and heat energy, or radiant energy, directly from the Sun. Energy is measured in joules. See also **kinetic energy**, **measure**, **potential energy**, **power**.

environment

Environment is another word for the surroundings in which animals and plants live. This includes such things as the **air**, **water**, **soil** and the shape of the land, which all affect the lives of plants and animals. The environment of humans includes climate, buildings and plant life. People are affected by the environment in which they live.

enzyme

An enzyme is a special kind of **catalyst** that is produced by a living cell. For instance, different enzymes control the different stages of **digestion**.

equilibrium

Equilibrium means a state of balance. It is used to describe something that does not change over a period of time.

evaporate

When a **liquid** changes into a **vapour** because it has been heated but not boiled, it is said to evaporate. On a sunny day a puddle soon dries up because the water evaporates as it is warmed by the Sun's heat. Water also evaporates from oceans, seas, rivers, ponds and all wet surfaces because of the heat of the Sun.

evolution

Evolution is the way in which **plants** and **animals** gradually change over millions of years. Plants and animals have evolved from simple forms to their present day shapes and sizes. Scientists believe that birds evolved from reptiles about 400 million years ago, while the earliest horses were about the size of a terrier dog.

excretion

Excretion is the way by which **plants** and **animals** get rid of waste materials. Some plants excrete waste materials through their leaves or bark. In animals, waste material leaves through the skin, or lungs, or kidneys.

birds
(have evolved)

exosphere

See **atmosphere**.

expand

When something becomes larger or spreads out, it is said to expand. Most **solids**, **liquids** and **gases** expand when they are heated. The opposite of expand is **contract**. Some thermometers have a liquid inside them which expands up the scale when heated.

Diagram showing evolution and extinction of different kinds of animals.

dinosaurs
(now extinct)

experiment

An experiment is a test carried out in order to discover whether something is true, or to find out something new. Scientists carry out experiments to help them understand how things work or behave.

extinct

Extinct means not existing any more. Dinosaurs are extinct reptiles. It is believed that 99 per cent of all the animal **species** that have ever lived are now extinct.

Extinction is now occurring faster than ever, mainly because people destroy the places where plants and animals live.

early reptile

F

fat

A fat is a greasy substance that does not dissolve in water. Fats, such as butter, lard and margarine, are usually **solids** at room temperature. Fats that are **liquids** at room temperature are called **oils**.

Fat is found in the bodies of animals and in plant seeds. It is an important food for animals because it is rich in **energy**. Fat under the skin also keeps an animal warm. However, eating too much fat can make you unhealthy.

fertilization

Fertilization is the joining together of male and female sex **cells**. Fertilization is the start of a new living thing. The **egg** cells in a female animal are fertilized by the male sperm cells. In plants, the egg cells in a flower are fertilized by male cells from the pollen grain.

fibre

A fibre is a long thin strand or thread of a material.

Linen, cotton and hemp are natural fibres which come from plants. Wool and silk are natural fibres obtained from animals. Nylon, rayon, polyester and fibreglass are just a few of the many examples of artificial, or synthetic, fibres.

Fibre is the name given to plant material that humans cannot digest. It is a very important part of our food since it absorbs water as it passes through the body. This helps to make the solid waste in the gut soft and bulky and easier to get rid of as faeces.

fibre optics

Fibre optics is the study of the passage of light along strong, fine, bendable glass fibres. See also **light**.

filter

A filter is something used for removing dust, dirt or other insoluble solids from a liquid or gas. The filter is made from a material which is full of tiny holes. The holes allow a liquid or gas to pass through, but not the larger particles of a solid.

Another meaning of filter is a transparent material, usually coloured, which is placed over the glass of a lamp or the lens of a camera. The filter changes the light by removing certain colours from it.

light

optical fibre

Light shining at the end of a bunch of optical fibres.

A full tanker is lower in the water than an empty one

A tanker floats as it is lighter than the sea underneath it.

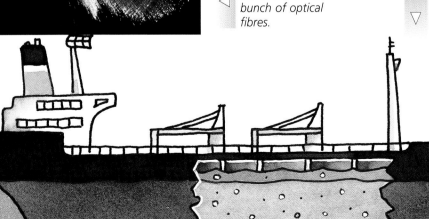

neutrons and energy released

fire

Fire is the heat and bright light that comes from **burning** things. Burning is a chemical process. Whatever you burn, whether it is a liquid like paraffin or a solid like coal or wood, it must be turned into a **gas** before it will burn. The gas combines with oxygen in the air and produces lots of heat and tiny pieces of carbon, called soot, and light which we call flames.

nucleus of atom

fission

In physics, fission is the splitting up of the nucleus of an **atom**. This gives a huge amount of **energy** and neutrons. Some power stations use nuclear fission to make **electricity**. In biology, fission is a form of reproduction in simple organisms. See also **power.**

neutron

In fission a neutron is used to hit another nucleus which then splits and releases energy.

float

To float is to stay or move on the surface of a **liquid** or in the **air**. An object will float only if it is lighter, or less dense, than the liquid in which it is suspended. In the case of water, something will float if each cubic centimetre of it weighs less than a cubic centimetre of water. This works for all other liquids and **gases** as well. Some things are so light that they can even float in air. **Helium**-filled balloons and hot-air balloons can float in air. See also **sink.**

fluid

A fluid is any substance that flows easily. **Liquids**, such as water, petrol and oil are fluids, so are **gases** such as air, oxygen and carbon dioxide. Unlike **solids**, fluids do not have a definite shape. They take up the shape of the container in which they are placed.

food

A food is anything that a plant or animal takes into its body to make itself **grow** or give it **energy**. Food also provides the materials the body needs to repair wounds and worn-out parts, and to keep it healthy.

food chain

A food chain is a series of living things that depend on each other for food **energy**. Each living thing in the food chain can be food for the next one. All food chains begin with green **plants**. These are the only living things able to make their own food. They do this by **photosynthesis**. Plant-eating animals, or **herbivores**, get their energy by eating plants. Then herbivores are eaten by flesh-eating animals, or **carnivores**, which may themselves be eaten by other carnivores.

Animals usually feed on many different foods. They, in turn, are eaten by many other animals. This is called a food chain.

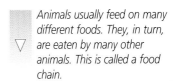

force

A force is any kind of push or pull. We cannot see a force, only what it does. A force can make a still thing move. It can make a moving thing travel faster, more slowly or in a different direction. A force may stop a moving object altogether.

Together, two or more forces can make something bend, stretch, squash, twist or turn. **Gravity**, wind, flowing water, magnetism and **friction** are some common forces.

Scientists measure forces in newtons. It takes a force of about 5 newtons to switch on a light and 20 newtons to open a drinks can.
See also **magnet, measure.**

Climbers use boots that give a large force of friction between their boots and the rock face.

formula

A formula is a shorthand way of writing scientific or mathematical information, using symbols, numbers and signs. Every **element** has a symbol and chemical formulae are used as shorthand for chemical compounds. Scientists use the formula H_2O for water as a molecule of water is made up of two atoms of **hydrogen** (H) for every one of **oxygen** (O). Table sugar has the formula $C_{12}H_{22}O_{11}$, while table salt is NaCl.

Friction from car tyres gives a driver a good grip on the road.

fossil

A fossil is the hardened remains, or shape, of a living thing preserved in rock. The commonest sorts of fossils show the hard parts of ancient plants and animals. From fossils we can learn about the plants and animals that lived millions of years ago and are now extinct, like the trilobite shown here. We can also find out about the way in which living things have gradually changed, or evolved, to their modern shape, size and way of life. From fossils we know that the first birds were around about 200 million years ago. The earliest fossils are just specks of carbon, 3500 million years old. They were found in western Australia.
See also **evolution**

fossil fuel

A fossil fuel is a **fuel** such as **coal**, **oil** or **natural gas.** They are called fossil fuels because they were formed from the remains of living things millions of years ago.

freeze

When a **liquid** changes to a **solid** because it is cooled, it is said to freeze. Different substances freeze at different temperatures. Pure water freezes to form ice at 0°C (degrees Celsius). A pure substance always freezes at the same temperature, called its freezing point. While the freezing point of pure water is 0°C, that of iron is 1540°C and that of oxygen is -183°C.
See also **boiling.**

frequency

Frequency is the number of complete cycles that happen in a repeating process in one second. For example, the number of radio waves passing a point in one second is the frequency of the radio waves. Frequency is measured in hertz. See also **wavelength**.

▷ *Friction is helpful when you ride a bike.*

friction

Friction is a kind of **force**. It occurs where moving objects or surfaces rub together. Friction slows down movement and produces **heat**. If you throw a ball, the ball has to 'slide' through the air. This causes a kind of friction called air resistance.

Meteors entering the Earth's atmosphere from outer space are burnt up by the heat produced by the rubbing effect, or friction, of the air.

Rough surfaces have more friction than smooth surfaces. **Oil** is used to reduce the friction between the moving parts of a machine and to stop wear and overheating. Friction can be very useful. It lets our feet grip the ground as we walk. Car and bicycle tyres grip the road and their brakes work because of friction.

friction helps tyres grip the road

friction with the air slows you down

friction helps your hands grip the handlebars

friction helps your feet grip the pedals

friction stops you when you put the brakes on

nucleus of atom (deuterium)

fuel

A fuel is a material that is burned to produce **heat** or other forms of **energy**. Most of the world's energy comes from **fossil fuels**. Nevertheless, wood is the main fuel for about 2 billion people in the world today.

nucleus of atom (tritium)

Nuclear fusion takes place when two nuclei join to form one.

nuclei of atoms join

fuse

A fuse is a safety device. It contains a short piece of thin wire that melts if too much **electricity** passes through it.

atom of helium and energy released

fusion

Fusion, or nuclear fusion, is the joining together of a **nucleus** from one **atom** with the nucleus of another atom (or the nuclei of several other atoms). This gives a much heavier nucleus. When this happens a huge amount of **energy** is released. The explosion of an atom bomb happens because of fusion.

neutron

G

gamma rays

See **radiation**.

gas

A gas is a substance like **air**, which weighs something but does not have a shape. A gas expands to take the shape of any container in which it is placed. Common gases include **oxygen**, **nitrogen** and **carbon dioxide**. See also **liquid**, **solid**.

gear

A gear is a set of toothed wheels in a **machine**. It is used to transmit motion from one part to another. In a car, gears take the **power** of the engine to the wheels. In a bicycle, gears alter the speed at which you have to pedal.

▷
A gear with a large sprocket means that the force is greater than with a small sprocket making it easier to go up a hill.

sprockets

gene

A gene is a small part of a **chromosome**. Genes carry the plans for making new plants and animals similar to their parents. There are, for example, genes for eye colour, hair colour and the colour of flowers. Chromosomes, and the genes they carry, are made of the substance called **DNA**. They are found in the **nucleus** of every **cell**.

generator

A generator is a **machine** for changing movement, or mechanical energy, into **electricity**. A bicycle dynamo is a small generator which is turned by the bicycle wheel. It produces electricity to work the cycle's lights. Mains electricity comes from huge **generators** turned by steam in **power** stations.

genetics

Genetics is finding out about **genes**. A geneticist is a scientist who answers such questions as: Why do tall parents often have tall children? Why does a baby chicken, and not a baby duck, hatch from a hen's egg?

geology

Geology is the study of the Earth's crust, its rocks, **soils**, **fossils** and **minerals**. Geologists are scientists who study how the continents, mountains, valleys and oceans were formed. They also study how the surface of the Earth, and the animals and plants which live on it, have changed during the millions of years since the Earth was formed.

pedal

chainwheel

chain

△ *Gears let a cyclist pedal with the same effort to go uphill as on level ground.*

geothermal power

See **power**.

▷ *On the Moon the force of gravity is less than that on Earth.*

germ

A germ is a very tiny living thing that causes disease or illness. Harmful **bacteria** and **viruses** are germs.

global warming

Global warming means the warming of the Earth's climate caused by an increased **greenhouse effect**.

gold

Gold is a heavy, yellow **metal**. It is an **element** that does not **rust** or tarnish. Because it is beautiful and rare, gold is a precious metal. It is used in coins, jewellery, ornaments, for repairing teeth and in the electronics industry. About 100 tonnes of gold-bearing rock have to be mined to produce just 1 kilogram of gold.

These are nuggets of naturally occurring gold found in soil deposits.

gram (g)

See **measure**.

gravity

Gravity is the invisible **force** which makes things you drop fall to the ground. A stone thrown up into the air will fall to the ground because it is pulled down by the Earth's gravity. The bigger the object, the larger the pull of gravity. Gravity pulling down gives people and objects **weight**.

The force of gravity decreases the further you are away from the centre of the **Earth**. The **Moon** and every other object in the **universe** also has gravity. Because it is smaller than the Earth, the Moon's gravity is less. On the Moon you would weigh only about a sixth of what you weigh on Earth. You would also be able to jump six times as high. The **Sun's** gravity attracts the Earth and other **planets** and holds them in their **orbits** so that they do not drift off into space.

greenhouse effect

The greenhouse effect is what happens when the **atmosphere** traps heat and causes the Earth to warm up. Without the greenhouse effect the Earth would be much colder than it is now. However, a more than usual amount of certain gases in the atmosphere from burning **fossil fuels** may lead to **global warming**. The main gases that trap heat are carbon dioxide and methane.

On average, world **temperatures** have risen by half a degree Celsius (°C) over the last 100 years. They could rise by another 3°C over the next 50 years. This could cause drought in some parts of the world, so that crops will not grow. Other areas could flood as the ice around the North and South Poles begins to melt and makes the sea-levels rise.

When the atmosphere traps heat and causes the Earth to warm up, this is called the greenhouse effect.

heat from the Sun

heat lost

heat trapped

grow

To grow is to become larger in size or to develop. All living things are able to grow with the help of **food**. They get bigger by making more **cells**.

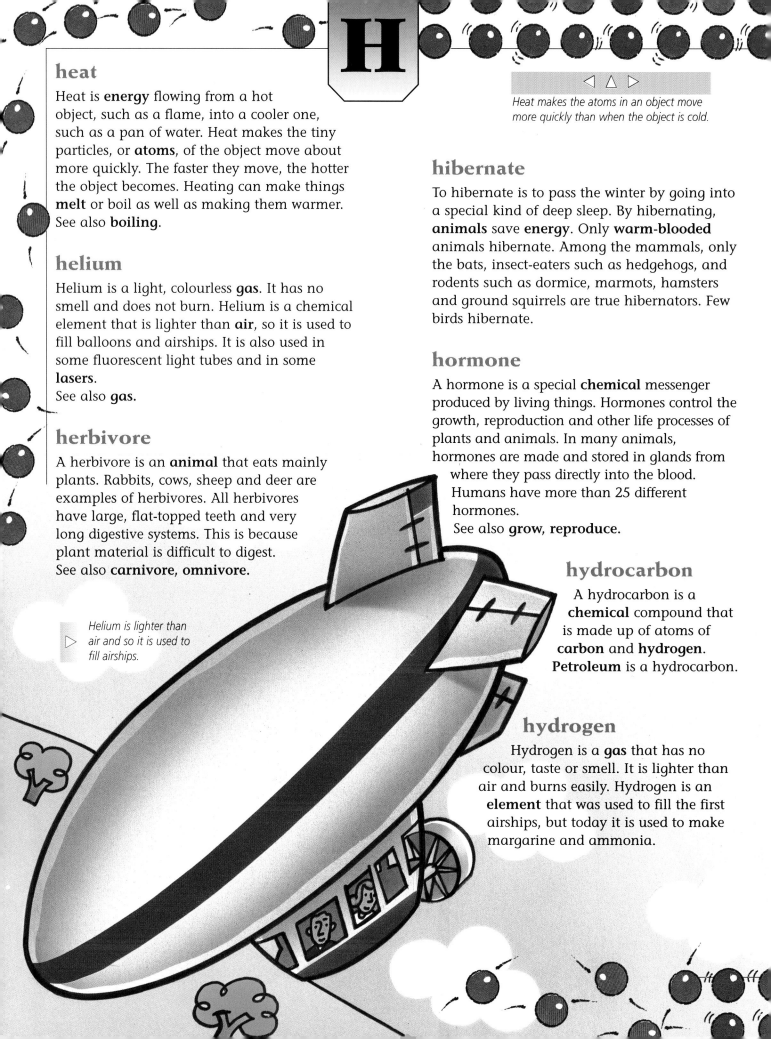

heat

Heat is **energy** flowing from a hot object, such as a flame, into a cooler one, such as a pan of water. Heat makes the tiny particles, or **atoms**, of the object move about more quickly. The faster they move, the hotter the object becomes. Heating can make things **melt** or boil as well as making them warmer.
See also **boiling**.

Heat makes the atoms in an object move more quickly than when the object is cold.

helium

Helium is a light, colourless **gas**. It has no smell and does not burn. Helium is a chemical element that is lighter than **air**, so it is used to fill balloons and airships. It is also used in some fluorescent light tubes and in some **lasers**.
See also **gas**.

herbivore

A herbivore is an **animal** that eats mainly plants. Rabbits, cows, sheep and deer are examples of herbivores. All herbivores have large, flat-topped teeth and very long digestive systems. This is because plant material is difficult to digest.
See also **carnivore, omnivore**.

▷ *Helium is lighter than air and so it is used to fill airships.*

hibernate

To hibernate is to pass the winter by going into a special kind of deep sleep. By hibernating, **animals** save **energy**. Only **warm-blooded** animals hibernate. Among the mammals, only the bats, insect-eaters such as hedgehogs, and rodents such as dormice, marmots, hamsters and ground squirrels are true hibernators. Few birds hibernate.

hormone

A hormone is a special **chemical** messenger produced by living things. Hormones control the growth, reproduction and other life processes of plants and animals. In many animals, hormones are made and stored in glands from where they pass directly into the blood. Humans have more than 25 different hormones.
See also **grow, reproduce**.

hydrocarbon

A hydrocarbon is a **chemical** compound that is made up of atoms of **carbon** and **hydrogen**. **Petroleum** is a hydrocarbon.

hydrogen

Hydrogen is a **gas** that has no colour, taste or smell. It is lighter than air and burns easily. Hydrogen is an **element** that was used to fill the first airships, but today it is used to make margarine and ammonia.

ice

Ice is **water** that has been frozen solid. Pure water **freezes** at 0°C (degrees Celsius). The temperature at which water freezes can be made lower by dissolving other substances in it. When water freezes into ice, it expands and takes up more space. Ice is less dense than water and light enough to float in it. See also **antifreeze**.

insoluble

See **dissolve**.

All branches of science depend on instruments for measuring and recording information.

instrument

A scientific instrument is a device for measuring or recording information. A thermometer, for example, is an instrument that measures temperature.

Another meaning of instrument is a tool used for delicate or scientific work, such as a pair of forceps.
See also **measure**.

insulate

To insulate is to cover something so as to reduce or stop the movement of **heat**, **sound** or **electricity**. A tea-cosy on a tea-pot is an insulator. Electricity cables are insulated with rubber or plastic. Double-glazed windows and doors have a layer of air, a good insulator, between the two layers of glass. Double-glazing reduces the loss of heat from a house and keeps noise out. Most non-metals, and all gases, are good heat insulators. Insulators are poor **conductors**.

micrometer

microscope

This marathon runner insulates himself with a shiny space blanket to stop him getting cold.

invertebrate

See **animal**.

ion

An ion is an **atom**, or a group of atoms, that has a positive or negative electric **charge**. Negative ions are formed by atoms gaining **electrons**, and positive ions are formed by atoms losing electrons.

ionosphere

See **atmosphere**.

iron

Iron is a hard, grey **metal**. It is the metal we use most of all. Iron is an **element**, but when mixed with carbon and other metals it forms the **alloy** steel. Iron **rusts** and corrodes in moist air. **Magnets** attract it. Plants and animals need small quantities of iron, in the form of iron salts, in their bodies if they are to stay healthy. Pure iron is not found in the ground. It is always combined with other elements in the form of **ores**.

isotope

An isotope is an **atom** that is chemically the same as another atom of a different **element** but does not have the same number of **neutrons** in its nucleus.

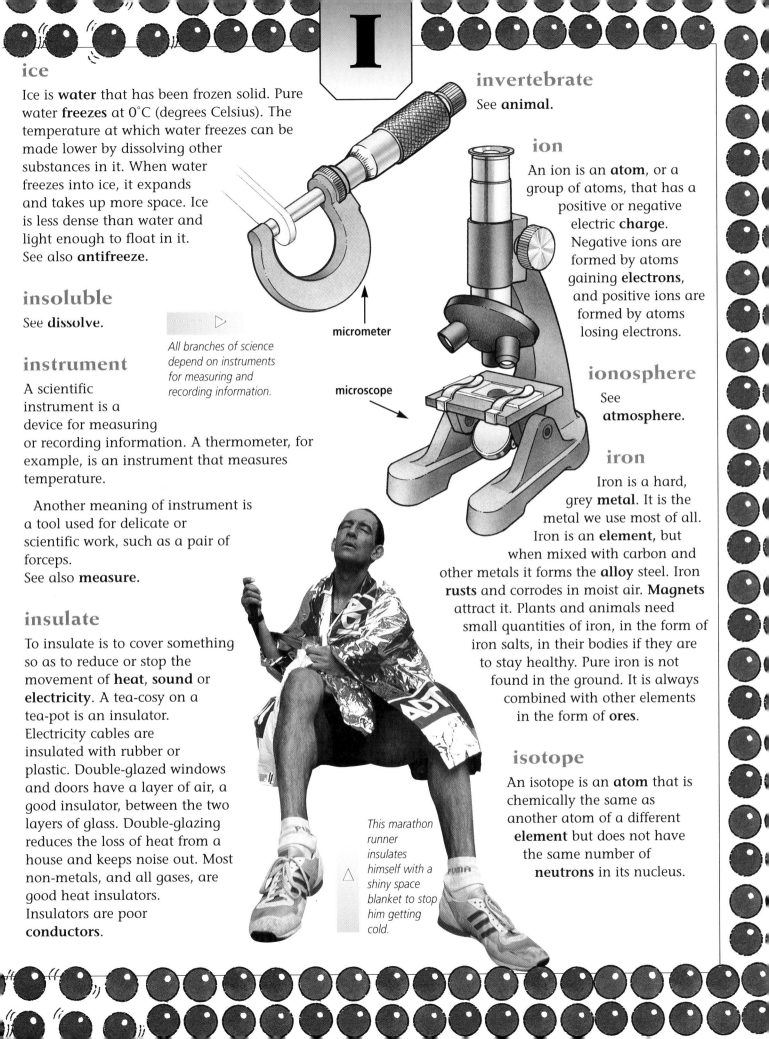

jet

A jet is a stream of liquid, gas or flame forced out of a narrow opening.

Jet is also a hard, black **mineral**.

joule (J)

See **measure**.

Jupiter

See **planet**.

kilogram (Kg)

See **measure**.

kilometre (Km)

See **measure**.

Laser waves are light waves that have the same wavelength and are all parallel to each other.

laser waves (light of same wavelength)

laser tube

atom

mirror

light from atom

light reflected from mirror

kinetic energy

Kinetic energy describes the **energy** of movement. Wind, flowing water and moving objects all have kinetic energy.
See also **potential energy**.

kingdom

A kingdom is one of the biggest groups into which living things are classified. Most scientists divide living things up into five kingdoms: the **animals**, **plants**, fungi, protists and monerans. Monerans have simple cells with no nucleus and protists have one cell only. Fungi are plant-like but live by absorbing food because they cannot make their own.
See also **classification**.

laboratory

A laboratory is the special room or building where scientists work. Scientists carry out **experiments** in a laboratory. It contains the equipment needed for scientific work.

laser

A laser is an instrument that produces a very bright, narrow beam of **light**. The beam is much narrower than an ordinary lamp and can be powerful enough to cut through **metal**.

Lasers are used in medicine to burn away birthmarks and some cancer cells. Many supermarket tills 'read' the bar codes on the things you buy with a laser. Compact disc players also use lasers to 'read' the contents of the disc.

lead

Lead is a soft, grey, heavy **metal**. It is a very useful **element**. **X-rays** and radioactive particles are absorbed by lead, so **radioactive** materials are stored in lead containers. In laboratories, hospitals and nuclear power stations, lead is used to protect workers from **radiation**. Car batteries contain lead plates, and this metal is used for making **alloys**.

Lead is poisonous and, used carelessly, it can cause **pollution** of the air, water and soil. The writing substance in the middle of a pencil is also known as 'lead'. Really it is a form of **carbon** called graphite.

lens

A lens is a piece of transparent glass or plastic with curved sides. Lenses can be used to make things look bigger or smaller. This is because **light** rays passing through a lens are bent, or refracted.

Spectacles, cameras, telescopes and binoculars have lenses. However, the lenses we use most often are the convex ones in our eyes. Each of these lenses focuses an image on the back of the eye.

lever

A lever is a simple **machine**. It is used for lifting weights, prising something open or turning an object. All levers consist of a strong, stiff bar that turns about a pivot, like a see-saw or a crowbar. You push or pull at one end of the lever and the weight is lifted at the other end. Some levers are used in pairs – scissors, pliers, shears and nutcrackers are all pairs of levers with a single pivot. Most levers put out more force than you put in, and so they make work easier.

life cycle

A life cycle is the series of changes through which a living thing passes as it grows from a fertilized egg to an adult. Some animals change their appearance by **metamorphosis** during their life cycle.
See also **fertilization**.

You can use a convex lens to make things look bigger or to make them look upside down!

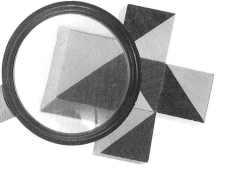

A concave lens always makes things look smaller.

light

Light is a kind of **radiation** which travels at very high speed. It comes from the **Sun**, electric lights or from hot or **burning** things, such as candles and fires.

White light is really a mixture of colours, each with a different **wavelength**. If white light is passed through a triangular piece of glass or clear plastic, called a prism, it breaks up into its separate colours. These are called the colours of the spectrum. A rainbow is really a spectrum in the sky. Rainbows are formed when the Sun shines while it is raining. Each raindrop acts as a tiny prism, splitting up the sunlight into the various colours.

Light travels in straight lines. The straight paths along which light travels are called rays. Light travels very fast. Rays of sunlight travel through space at almost 300000 kilometres a second. When light rays hit a shiny surface, such as a **mirror**, they bounce off or are reflected. The **Moon** shines because it reflects sunlight.

If an **opaque** object stands in the way of rays of light, a dark shape, or shadow, forms behind it.

When light rays pass through a clear, or **transparent**, substance, they slow down and are bent slightly. This bending is called refraction. A pencil or drinking straw seems to bend in a glass of water. This is because the light rays are bent, or refracted, when they pass from the air into water. **Lenses** and prisms work because light rays are bent or refracted when they pass from the air into transparent glass or plastic.
See also **colour**.

① *Light bounces off a mirror.*

② *It is bent when it passes through a clear substance.*

③ *It breaks up into separate colours when it passes through a prism.*

M

limestone

See **chalk**.

liquid

A liquid is a substance that can flow, like water or oil. In still conditions, a liquid always has a level surface and it takes the shape of any container in which it is placed.
See also **gas, solid**.

litre (L)

See **measure**.

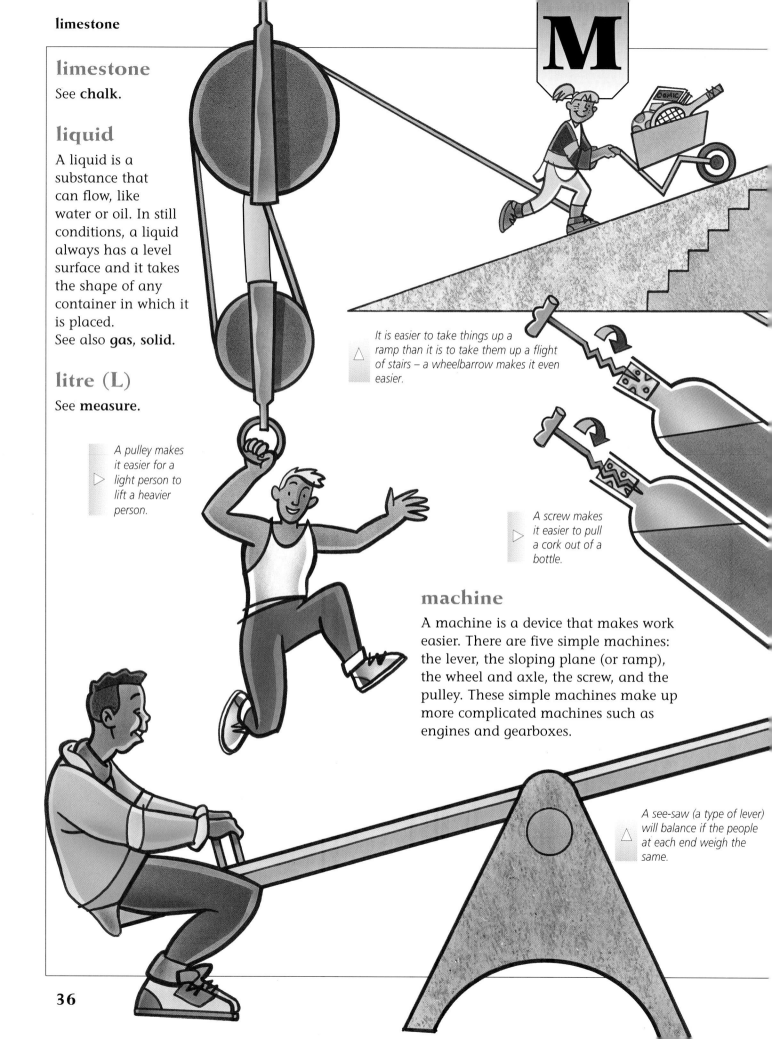

A pulley makes it easier for a light person to lift a heavier person.

It is easier to take things up a ramp than it is to take them up a flight of stairs – a wheelbarrow makes it even easier.

A screw makes it easier to pull a cork out of a bottle.

machine

A machine is a device that makes work easier. There are five simple machines: the lever, the sloping plane (or ramp), the wheel and axle, the screw, and the pulley. These simple machines make up more complicated machines such as engines and gearboxes.

A see-saw (a type of lever) will balance if the people at each end weigh the same.

magnet

A magnet attracts iron and things containing **iron**. Magnets are made from magnetic materials. **Nickel**, cobalt, iron and **steel** are all magnetic materials.

The space around a magnet, in which its **force** acts, is called a magnetic field. A magnet will attract or repel other magnets. When it is hung in the air, a magnet will always point in a north–south direction. Most magnetism is concentrated at the ends, or poles, which we call north (N) and south (S). Magnets lose their magnetism if they are heated, dropped or hit.

Magnets are found in electric motors, generators, compasses, loudspeakers, magnetic tape and many other electrical devices.

The world's heaviest magnet is at a research station at Dubna in the former Soviet Union. It weighs 36 000 tonnes.

An electromagnet is a type of magnet which can be switched on and off because it uses an electric **current** to work.

magnifying glass

A magnifying glass is a convex **lens** that is used to make objects look larger.

Mars

See **planet**.

mass

Mass is a measure of how much **matter** there is in an object. All objects have mass and take up space. Mass is measured in kilograms. It is not the same as **weight**. This is because the mass of an object always remains the same, even in space. The weight of an object in space is less than on Earth. This is because the pull of **gravity** is less.
See also **measure**.

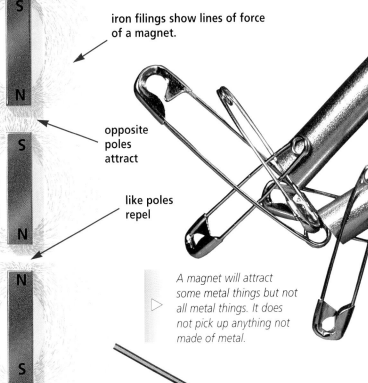

The force of a magnet is called its magnetic field. The force comes from the north (N) and south (S) poles of the magnets.

material

Material is any matter from which other things can be made. Natural materials include those from plants, such as wood and cork, and those from animals, like leather, bone or wool. Sand, stone, clay and iron ore are also natural materials. Artificial, or synthetic, materials are made by mixing natural materials together and changing them. Many artificial materials, such as plastic, are made by mixing chemicals which have been made from coal or oil.

iron filings show lines of force of a magnet.

opposite poles attract

like poles repel

A magnet will attract some metal things but not all metal things. It does not pick up anything not made of metal.

matter

Matter is the material of which all things in the universe are made. **Solids, liquids** and **gases** are three types, or states, of matter. Your body is a mixture of all three. Your teeth, muscles and bones are solid, the main part of your blood is liquid, while there is a gas (air) in your lungs.

Measure

We measure something to find out how big it is, such as when we measure the width of a door to see if a desk will go through it.

A measure is a unit of size, time, volume or some other quantity. We might, for example, buy a litre of milk. A litre is a measure of volume.

Another meaning of measure is a device, such as a ruler, which we use for measuring.

You can get a friend to measure your height by marking a vertical ruler level with the top of your head.

early measurements

When people first started measuring things, they used parts of the body as a ruler. The ancient Egyptians measured in cubits. This was the distance from the elbow to the tip of the middle finger. The Romans measured distance in feet – the length of a Roman's foot. Unfortunately people's arms and feet are not all the same length. A standard was needed so that rulers could all measure in the same way.

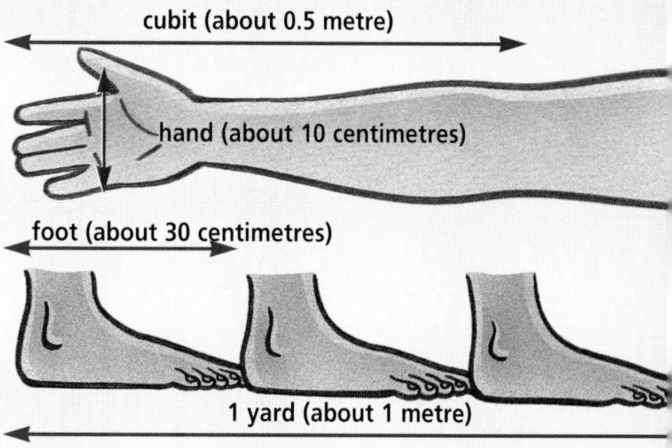

cubit (about 0.5 metre)

hand (about 10 centimetres)

foot (about 30 centimetres)

1 yard (about 1 metre)

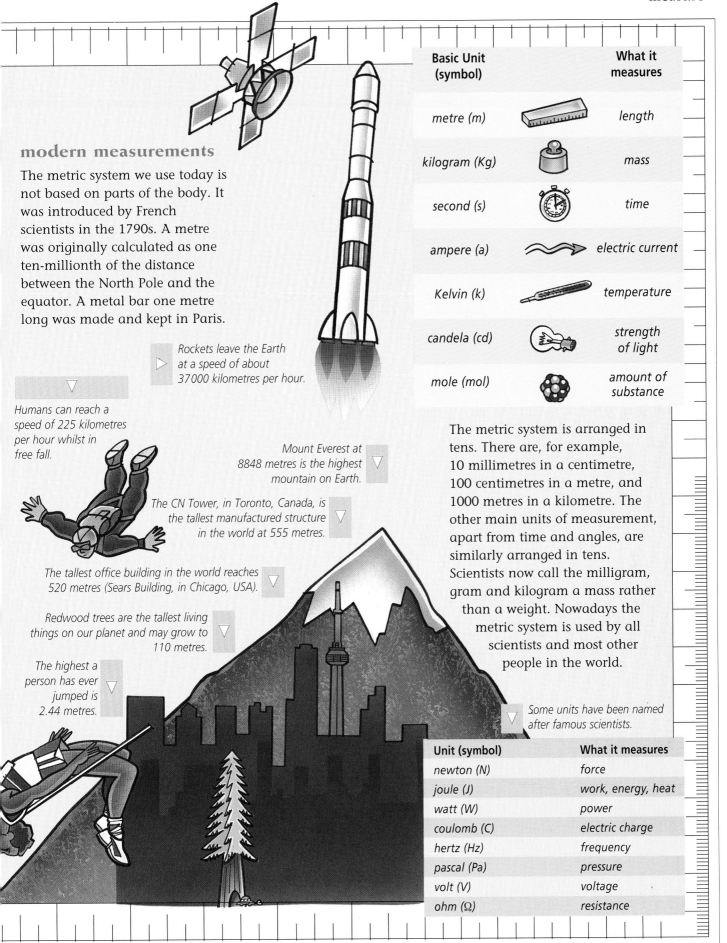

modern measurements

The metric system we use today is not based on parts of the body. It was introduced by French scientists in the 1790s. A metre was originally calculated as one ten-millionth of the distance between the North Pole and the equator. A metal bar one metre long was made and kept in Paris.

Rockets leave the Earth at a speed of about 37000 kilometres per hour.

Humans can reach a speed of 225 kilometres per hour whilst in free fall.

Mount Everest at 8848 metres is the highest mountain on Earth.

The CN Tower, in Toronto, Canada, is the tallest manufactured structure in the world at 555 metres.

The tallest office building in the world reaches 520 metres (Sears Building, in Chicago, USA).

Redwood trees are the tallest living things on our planet and may grow to 110 metres.

The highest a person has ever jumped is 2.44 metres.

Basic Unit (symbol)		What it measures
metre (m)		length
kilogram (Kg)		mass
second (s)		time
ampere (a)		electric current
Kelvin (k)		temperature
candela (cd)		strength of light
mole (mol)		amount of substance

The metric system is arranged in tens. There are, for example, 10 millimetres in a centimetre, 100 centimetres in a metre, and 1000 metres in a kilometre. The other main units of measurement, apart from time and angles, are similarly arranged in tens. Scientists now call the milligram, gram and kilogram a mass rather than a weight. Nowadays the metric system is used by all scientists and most other people in the world.

Some units have been named after famous scientists.

Unit (symbol)	What it measures
newton (N)	force
joule (J)	work, energy, heat
watt (W)	power
coulomb (C)	electric charge
hertz (Hz)	frequency
pascal (Pa)	pressure
volt (V)	voltage
ohm (Ω)	resistance

mechanical energy

See **energy**.

medicine

Medicine is finding out about healing and preventing disease. Doctors study medicine.

A medicine is a substance usually swallowed or injected to treat illness or pain.

melt

To melt is to change a solid into a liquid by heating it. We melt ice into water if we warm it. Metals are melted by heating them in furnaces. The temperature at which a solid starts to melt is called its melting point. The melting point of pure ice is 0°C (degrees Celsius), and that of tungsten is 3387°C.

melting point

See **melt**.

mercury

Mercury is a heavy, silver-coloured **metal**. It is sometimes called 'quicksilver' because it is a liquid at room temperature. It is used in many thermometers and in some electrical switches and long-life batteries. Mercury is an **element** that readily forms alloys, one of which is used by dentists for filling teeth. Pure mercury is poisonous and must be handled carefully.

A **planet** in our solar system is also called Mercury. It is the closest planet to the Sun.

△

These are drops of mercury.

adult butterfly lays eggs

pupa

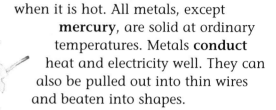
◁ *The life cycle of a butterfly includes metamorphosis from a caterpillar.*

caterpillar

eggs

metal

A metal is a shiny **mineral** that melts when it is hot. All metals, except **mercury**, are solid at ordinary temperatures. Metals **conduct** heat and electricity well. They can also be pulled out into thin wires and beaten into shapes.

Iron, **copper**, **gold** and **tin** are all metals. More than 70 of the chemical **elements** are metals. Certain metals can be melted together to form **alloys**. Most metals are obtained from **ores**. In Egypt as long ago as 4000 BC people discovered how to make copper from copper ore.

▽ ▷
The life cycle of a frog includes metamorphosis from a tadpole.

metamorphosis

Metamorphosis is the change in shape and form which some young animals go through during their **life cycle** before they become an adult. Butterflies and moths undergo metamorphosis. They change from an egg to a caterpillar, or larva, to a chrysalis, or pupa, then to an adult. Frogs and toads change from egg to tadpole to adult.

tadpole

tadpole grows legs

adult frog lays eggs and the cycle starts again

tail begins to disappear

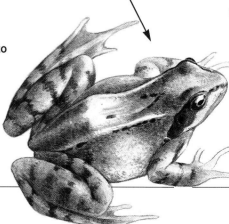

meter

A meter is an instrument or machine used for measuring. A gas meter, for example, measures the volume of gas you have used. A barometer measures the atmospheric pressure, while an altimeter measures the height above sea-level.
See also **measure**.

methane

See **gas**.

metre (m)

See **measure**.

metric system

See **measure**.

microbe

See **micro-organism**.

microchip

A microchip is another name for a **silicon** chip.

micro-organism

A micro-organism is a very small living thing that can be seen only with a **microscope**. **Bacteria** are micro-organisms. Microbe is another name for micro-organism.

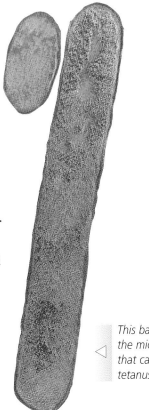

This is a microprocessor showing its two rows of terminals wired into an electronic circuit.

This bacterium is the micro-organism that causes tetanus.

microprocessor

A microprocessor is a tiny electronic computer built on a **silicon** chip. It is used in many electronic devices including calculators and most computers. Washing machines, video recorders and many other household machines are controlled by microprocessors.

microscope

A microscope is an **instrument** that uses two or more magnifying **lenses** to make tiny objects appear much larger. An electron microscope uses a beam of **electrons** instead of **light** to make objects many thousands of times larger. The first microscope was made in about 1600 by Zacharias Janssen (Holland, about 1570–1638).

microwave

A microwave is a radio **wave** with a very short **wavelength**. It is produced by an electronic device called a magnetron. In microwave ovens, food is cooked by the energy absorbed from microwaves. Telephone calls and TV programmes are sent long distances using microwaves transmitted by satellites. Radar also uses microwaves.

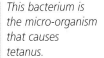

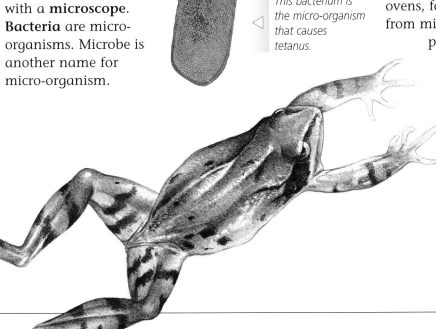

milligram (mg)

See **measure**.

millimetre (mm)

See **measure**.

mineral

A mineral is any natural material found in the ground that does not come from plants or animals. Minerals include everyday substances such as rock **salt**, **asbestos**, the graphite used as pencil 'lead', talc used to make talcum powder and the china clay used to make crockery. **Gold**, **silver** and **diamonds** are also minerals. Scientists have identified more than 2500 different minerals, but many of them are quite rare.

A mineral salt is a mineral substance living things need in order to stay alive. For example, iron salts are needed to make the red colouring in red blood cells, which carry **oxygen** around the body. Plant roots take up mineral salts dissolved in water from the **soil**.

△
This mirror has a mixture of concave and convex surfaces.

In the concave side (front) of a spoon, your image is upside down, unless you are very close to the spoon.

mirror

A mirror is a smooth piece of glass with a backing of silver, or another shiny metal, which reflects **light**. A flat mirror produces an image that appears to be as far behind the mirror as the object is in front. The image is always reversed left to right (a mirror image).

A concave mirror, such as the inside of the bowl of a spoon, produces an upright magnified image when you are close to it and an upside down (inverted), distorted image of distant objects.

A convex mirror, such as the back of the bowl of a spoon, produces an image that is the right way up but smaller. Convex mirrors also reflect more of their surroundings. They are used as car wing mirrors and as security mirrors in shops.

See also **lens**.

▷
In the convex side (back) of a spoon, the image is always right way up.

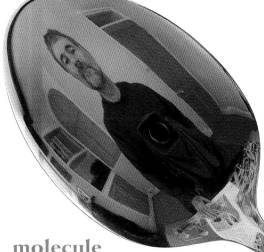

molecule

A molecule is a tiny particle of a substance. A molecule consists of two or more **atoms** held together by **bonds**. A molecule of **water**, for example, consists of two hydrogen atoms and one oxygen atom. Large molecules, such as **DNA**, consist of many hundreds of thousands of atoms.

moon

A moon is any natural satellite of any planet. Saturn, for example, has more than 20 moons circling it.

The **Earth**'s natural satellite is called the Moon. The Moon is made of rock and has no **atmosphere** and no **water**. It does not give out any **light** of its own but shines only because it reflects some of the sunlight falling on it.

The Moon orbits the Earth nearly once every month. The same part of the Moon always faces the Earth, although the amount of it that looks bright changes.

▷

The Moon is a massive round rock covered with craters.

motion

Motion is movement. Something is in motion when it moves from place to place. See also **force**.

motor

A motor is a **machine** that moves or causes movement. Motors use other kinds of **energy** to release mechanical energy, or motion. Electric motors, clockwork motors and internal combustion engines are different kinds of motor.

oxygen atom   hydrogen atoms

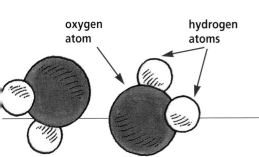

natural gas

Natural gas is the **gas** burned in cookers and central heating boilers. It was formed from the remains of tiny plants and animals that lived millions of years ago.
See also **fossil fuel**.

Neptune

See **planet**.

neutralize

To neutralize is to change a substance or solution so that it is neither an **acid** nor an **alkali**. An alkali in toothpaste, for example, helps to neutralize the acids in the mouth which cause tooth decay.

neutron

A neutron is one of the tiny particles found in the **nucleus** of an **atom**. **Hydrogen** is the only **element** that does not have neutrons in its atoms.

newton

See **measure**.

nickel

Nickel is a hard, silvery-white **metal**. It is an **element** that is used to coat other metals to stop them rusting or corroding. It is also one of the metals commonly used in **alloys**. An alloy of nickel and copper is used for making coins.

nitrogen

Nitrogen is a **gas** that occurs in the **atmosphere**. Four-fifths of the **air** is nitrogen. It is an **element** that is essential to living things, for instance, all **proteins** contain nitrogen.

noise

See **sound**.

non-metal

A non-metal is any **element** that does not behave like a **metal**. It does not **conduct** heat or electricity well. A non-metal can be a **solid**, such as carbon, a **liquid** such as bromine, or a **gas** such as oxygen or nitrogen.

nuclear energy

See **energy**.

nucleus

The nucleus of an **atom** contains tiny particles called **protons** and **neutrons**. It is the breakdown of atomic nuclei that gives rise to **radioactivity**.

In biology, the nucleus is a structure found in most plant animal **cells**. The nucleus contains the **chromosomes** and controls the growth and reproduction of the cell. If the nucleus is damaged the cell dies.

nutrition

Nutrition describes the process of taking in and digesting **food**. It is a process carried out by all living organisms.

Oils come from plants such as sunflowers, olives, peanuts and lavender.

△

▽ *Oil was formed from the remains of plants and tiny sea creatures which died many millions of years ago.*

ohm

See **measure**.

oil

An oil is a thick, slippery or greasy **liquid** that does not mix with water. Oils **burn** readily, with a smoky flame. They are obtained from certain plants and animals and also from the Earth's crust.

Vegetable oils are obtained by crushing seeds or heating them in steam. Olive oil, palm oil, coconut oil and linseed oil are obtained in this way. Some oils from flowers are used in making perfumes, for example lavender oil.

Cod liver oil and halibut oil, which are rich in vitamins A and D, are obtained from the fish cod and halibut.

Petrol, diesel oil and kerosene are obtained from deposits of mineral oil or crude oil under the surface of the Earth. This oil is the remains of tiny plants and animals which lived in the sea millions of years ago. Petroleum oil is a good lubricant. It is put on the moving parts of machines to reduce **friction** and so help the parts to move more freely.
See also **fossil fuel, petroleum**.

omnivore

An omnivore is an animal that eats both plants and animals. Badgers and most humans are omnivores.
See also **carnivore, herbivore**.

oil   gas

opaque

Opaque describes a material or object that you cannot see through because **light** does not pass through it. Wood and metal are opaque.
See also **light**.

orbit

An orbit is the path of a **planet**, satellite or **moon** as it moves around the Earth or some other body in space.

The path taken by an **electron** as it moves around the **nucleus** of an **atom** is also called an orbit.

ore

An ore is any **mineral** found in the Earth from which **metals** can be obtained. **Iron**, for example, is obtained from a reddish-brown ore called haematite.

organ

An organ is a part of the body which has a particular job to do. The brain, liver and kidneys are all organs.

Crude oil is used to make many substances.
petrol
plastics
rubber
diesel
fuel
waxes
oils

organism

An organism is a living thing. Seaweed, otters, sticklebacks, bees, bacteria and fungi are all organisms.

oxygen

Oxygen is a **gas** that occurs in the atmosphere. One-fifth of the **air** is oxygen. Oxygen has no colour, taste or smell. It is an **element** which all plants and animals need to live. Also, **fuels** need oxygen to burn.

ozone

Ozone is a pale blue **gas** with a sharp smell. It is a form of **oxygen** and occurs naturally in the upper part of the Earth's **atmosphere**. This ozone forms a layer that filters out dangerous rays from the Sun. Scientists believe that some kinds of air **pollution** are destroying the ozone layer. This could cause an increase in skin cancer and also damage crop plants.

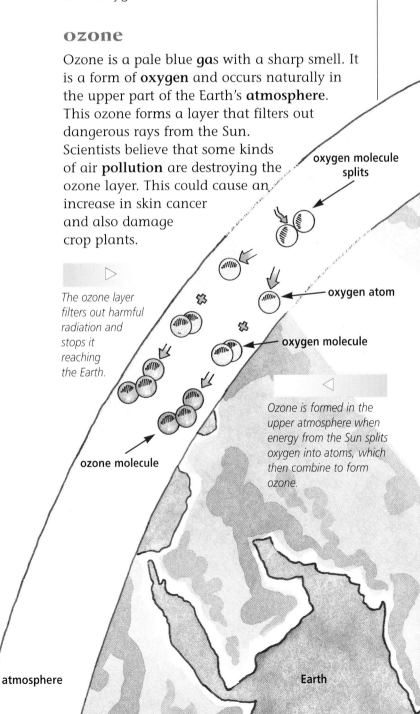

oxygen molecule splits

oxygen atom

oxygen molecule

The ozone layer filters out harmful radiation and stops it reaching the Earth.

ozone molecule

Ozone is formed in the upper atmosphere when energy from the Sun splits oxygen into atoms, which then combine to form ozone.

atmosphere

Earth

P Q

particle

A particle is one of the tiny simple parts of which all **matter** is made. **Electrons, neutrons** and **protons** are examples of particles.

pasteurize

To pasteurize is to heat a liquid to kill harmful **bacteria**. Most milk is pasteurized. The process was named after the scientist Louis Pasteur (France, 1822–1895), who invented it. See also **sterilize**.

▷ *Some substances change colour throughout the pH range from 0 to 14. These substances are used as indicators to show the pH of a substance.*

battery acid

milk of magnesia

soap

rain

vinegar

apple juice

lemon juice

pure water

oven cleaner

pH 14

bleach

pH 1

pendulum

A pendulum is a weight hanging from a thread, chain or rod. A pendulum can swing freely to and fro. The length of a pendulum affects how long it takes to swing. A short pendulum takes less time for each swing than a long pendulum. Pendulums are used in many large clocks to regulate the toothed gears that move the hands.

salt water

period

A period is a length of time, or the time for one swing of a pendulum or other similar repeating process.

petroleum

Petroleum is a dark oily liquid which is found beneath the Earth's surface. It is sometimes called crude oil.
See also **oil**.

pH

pH is a measure of how like an **acid** or how like an **alkali** a solution is. A very strong acid has a pH of 1. A very strong alkali has a pH of 14. Pure water has a pH of 7 and is neither alkaline nor acid. It is said to be **neutral**.

photosynthesis

Photosynthesis is the way in which green **plants** make their own food. Green plants use sunlight to turn **carbon dioxide** and **water** into **carbohydrates** (sugars and starches) for food. Plants absorb sunlight using the green pigment, **chlorophyll**. Photosynthesis also releases **oxygen** gas, which all living things need. All other living things also depend on plants directly or indirectly for **food**.

physics

Physics is finding out about **space, matter, energy, heat, light, sound, electricity** and magnetism. A physicist is a scientist who studies and works in physics.

▷ *Plants make sugars and starches by photosynthesis. They need the green pigment chlorophyll to do this.*

sunlight

planet

A planet is any one of the nine large bodies in **space**, that revolve around the **Sun**. Our **Earth** is a planet. The names of the planets, moving outwards from the Sun are: Mercury, Venus, Earth, Mars, Jupiter, Saturn, Uranus, Neptune and Pluto.

Planets do not produce **light** of their own. They shine because they **reflect** sunlight. Some planets are balls of rock, like the Earth. Jupiter, Saturn, Uranus and Neptune are giant balls of **gas**. Many of the planets have natural satellites (**moons**) orbiting round them.

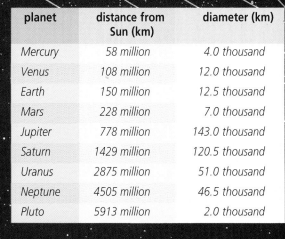

▷ The Sun's gravity holds the planets in orbit.

Sun

carbon dioxide

sugars and starches

oxygen

chlorophyll

planet	distance from Sun (km)	diameter (km)
Mercury	58 million	4.0 thousand
Venus	108 million	12.0 thousand
Earth	150 million	12.5 thousand
Mars	228 million	7.0 thousand
Jupiter	778 million	143.0 thousand
Saturn	1429 million	120.5 thousand
Uranus	2875 million	51.0 thousand
Neptune	4505 million	46.5 thousand
Pluto	5913 million	2.0 thousand

Plants

A plant is any member of the plant kingdom. All plants make their own food by **photosynthesis**. During this process they use the energy of sunlight to change simple substances into **food**. **Oxygen** is a waste product of photosynthesis. Like animals, plants grow, reproduce and respire. But unlike animals, plants cannot move from place to place. Because they do not have nerves, plants react slowly to changes in their surroundings.

Animals rely on the food made by plants. All animals either eat plants or they eat other animals which feed on plants. Without plants, all animals, including humans, would die.

algae

Algae live wherever there is water, light and mineral salts. The smallest algae are tiny, single-celled plants. They can be seen only with a microscope. The largest algae are seaweeds. They reproduce with spores.

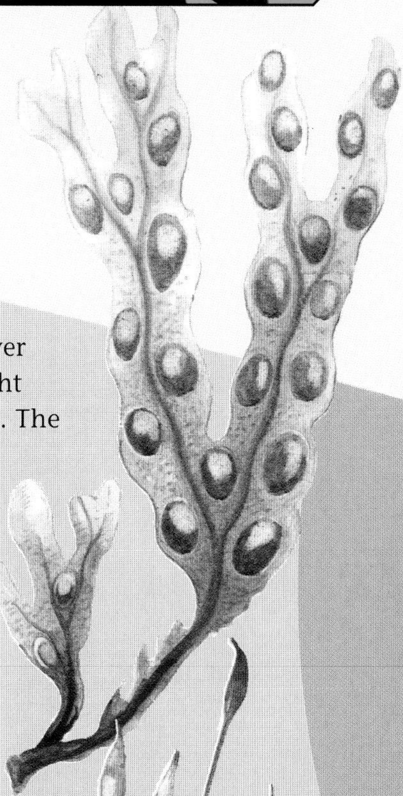

seaweed

mosses and liverworts

Mosses and liverworts are simple, green plants. They live in moist places on land. Liverworts have a ribbon-like or leafy shape. Mosses have leaf-like scales. Mosses and liverworts reproduce with spores.

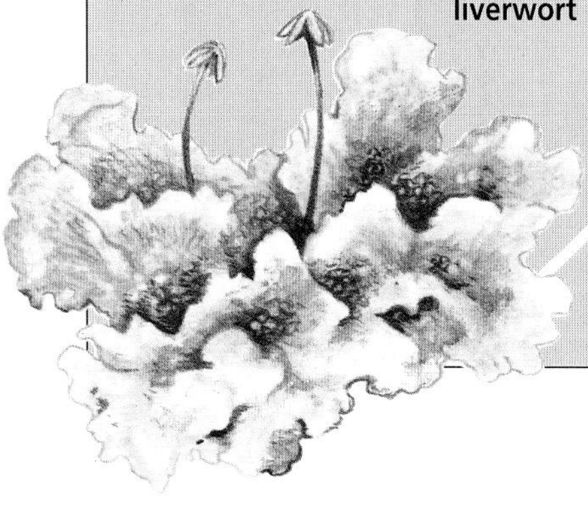

moss

liverwort

ferns

Ferns usually live in damp places on land. Ferns have leaves, or fronds, that are made up of many small leaflets. Ferns form spores on the underside of their leaves.

fern

fern

Algae

no roots, stems or leaves

produce spores

Mosses and Liverworts

simple leaves

produce spores

Ferns

roots, stems and leaves

produce spores

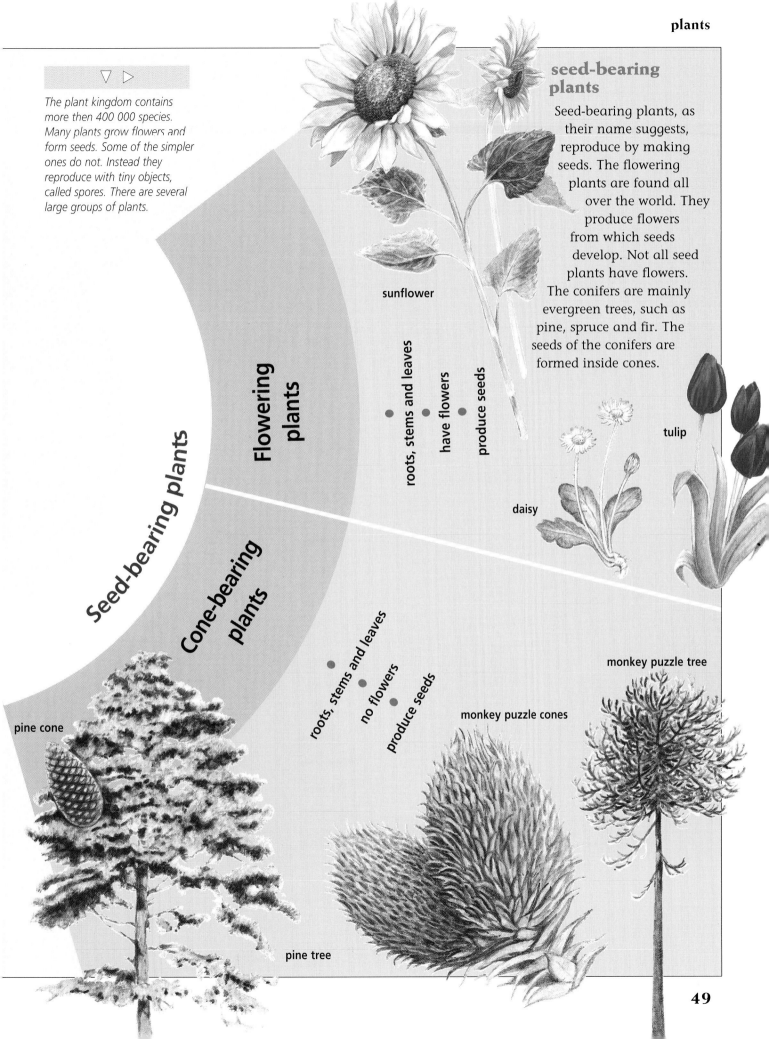

The plant kingdom contains more then 400 000 species. Many plants grow flowers and form seeds. Some of the simpler ones do not. Instead they reproduce with tiny objects, called spores. There are several large groups of plants.

seed-bearing plants

Seed-bearing plants, as their name suggests, reproduce by making seeds. The flowering plants are found all over the world. They produce flowers from which seeds develop. Not all seed plants have flowers. The conifers are mainly evergreen trees, such as pine, spruce and fir. The seeds of the conifers are formed inside cones.

sunflower

Seed-bearing plants

Flowering plants

roots, stems and leaves
have flowers
produce seeds

daisy

tulip

Cone-bearing plants

roots, stems and leaves
no flowers
produce seeds

monkey puzzle tree

monkey puzzle cones

pine cone

pine tree

49

plastic

A plastic is a strong, light, synthetic **material**. Plastics can be moulded into different shapes. Most plastics are made from **chemicals** found in **oil**, although a few come from **coal**, wood and natural gas. Common types of plastic include polythene, polystyrene, PVC and nylon.

Plastics do not **rust** or rot, and they can be made in almost every shape or colour. Most plastics do not allow **electricity** to pass through them. Because of this, they can be used to cover wires, plugs and other electrical items.

Some plastics are hard, others are soft and stretchy. Many plastics are **transparent**. Certain plastics can be filled with tiny bubbles of gas, to make plastic foam. Some can be drawn out into fine **fibres** and woven into cloth. Other plastics can be used to make glues and paints.

Pluto

See **planet**.

pole

See **magnet**.

pollution

Pollution means spoiling or dirtying a place or thing. Pollution can be caused by exhaust fumes from motor vehicles or smoke from factory chimneys. Chemical waste, nuclear waste and spilled oil can cause pollution. Sewage and carelessly used pesticides and fertilizers can cause pollution. Noise is also a form of pollution. See also **acid rain**.

△

An oil spill polluting a rocky coastline is washed off and then vacuumed up with hoses.

polymer

A polymer is any large **molecule** made up of lots of groups of the same **atoms**. Polythene is an example of a polymer.

potential energy

Potential energy is the **energy** present in something because of its position. For instance, the water behind a dam wall has huge amounts of potential energy. See also **kinetic energy**.

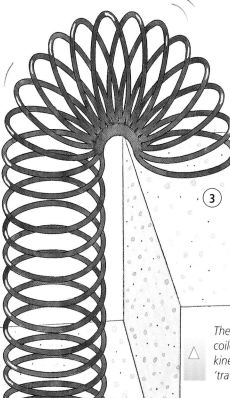

① *The coiled spring has potential energy when it is stationary.*
② *This becomes kinetic energy as it is flipped and* ③ *continues down the steps by itself.*

③

△ *The potential energy of the coiled spring changes to kinetic energy when it 'travels' down the steps.*

power

Power is the rate at which **energy** is turned from one form to another. The power of an engine is the rate at which it can drive a **machine**. It is often measured in units called kilowatts.

The power of a light bulb is the rate at which it can turn electrical energy into **light** and **heat**. This is measured in watts. A 1000 watt (1 kilowatt) electric fire uses energy ten times as fast as a 100 watt bulb. Because of this, it costs ten times as much to run for the same length of time.

A power station is a building or place where **electricity** is produced. Most power stations burn a **fuel**, such as coal, oil or gas to produce **heat**. This heat is used to turn water into steam. The steam rushing past the blades of a turbine makes it spin. As the turbine turns, so does the **generator**. The generator produces electricity.

A nuclear power station uses a **radioactive** material called uranium. A hydroelectric power station uses the energy of running water. A tidal power station uses the movement of the tides and a wave power station uses the waves of the sea. Sometimes the energy of the wind is used to produce electricity. Tall, slim wind turbines are turned by the wind to drive generators. Sometimes there are hot springs which shoot steam or hot water into the air. This geothermal power is used to produce electricity. Solar power stations change sunlight into electricity.

wind power   solar power   water power

turbine in power station
mains electricity

Power stations use energy to drive turbines to produce electricity.

pressure

Pressure is a **force** spread over an area. The pressure is large if a force is spread over a small area, and the pressure is small if the same force is spread over a larger area. Scientists **measure** pressure in newtons per square metre.

A balloon stays inflated because the pressure on the inside is greater than that on the outside.

primary colour

See **colour**.

prism

See **colour**, **light**.

protein

A protein is one of the basic kinds of biological **molecule** from which living things are made. Muscles contain protein and **enzymes** are proteins.

Living things need protein if they are to grow and repair parts of their bodies. Meat, milk, eggs, fish, beans and peas are foods rich in proteins. Proteins all contain **nitrogen**.

proton

A proton is one of the tiny particles in the **nucleus** of an **atom**.

pulley

A pulley is a simple **machine**. It consists of a grooved wheel, around which a rope or chain is pulled to raise a **weight**. If more than one pulley wheel is used on the same rope, a heavy weight can be lifted with a small amount of **force**.

pump

A pump is a device used to push or raise **liquids** or **gases**. The heart is a pump made of muscle. It pushes blood around the body.

purify

To purify is to make something clean or pure. A pure substance is one that is not mixed with other substances. Purifying is the method of removing unwanted materials or germs from air, water or other substances.

quartz

Quartz is a hard, transparent **mineral**. It is one of the commonest minerals of the Earth's crust. Quartz contains **silicon** and readily forms **crystals**.

Coloured forms of quartz are semi-precious stones, such as amethyst, agate and moonstone. They are used to make jewellery. Quartz crystals are also used in watches and clocks.

Sand is mostly made of quartz. It is used to make glass.

Quartz crystals are colourless when pure.

radiation

Radiation is the **energy** given out in the form of particles or **waves** from certain objects and materials.

We receive **heat** and **light** radiation from the Sun. Other forms of radiation include **X-ray** radiation and nuclear radiation.

See also **electromagnetic radiation**.

radioactive

A radioactive material is one that gives off harmful **radiation**. The radiation comes from unstable **atoms**. Uranium is a radioactive material. The radiation can be in the form of **waves** or tiny particles.

lead

aluminium

paper

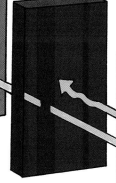
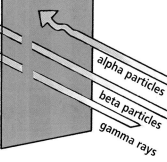

alpha particles

beta particles

gamma rays

rainbow

See **colour, light**.

ray

See **light**.

Some radioactive rays or particles are stopped by paper, others are only stopped by lead.

reaction

A reaction, or chemical reaction, is a process in which substances have an effect on each other and new substances are produced. When **iron** combines with **oxygen** in the presence of water then iron oxide, or **rust**, is formed.

recycling

Recycling is collecting and treating waste **materials** so that they can be used again. Recycling saves **energy**, materials and land. Waste paper, for example, can be made into new paper. Metals and glass are also used to make new metals and glass. Vegetable waste can be made into compost. If 75 per cent of the waste paper and cardboard we use was recycled and made into new paper and cardboard, 35 million trees could be saved each year.

Recycling takes scrap metals, glass bottles, paper, cloth and aluminium cans and treats them so they can be used again.

reflection

See **light**.

There are many forms of radiation, including light from the Sun.

refraction

See **light**.

reproduce

To reproduce is to produce young or offspring. Reproduction means that a **species** of plant, animal, fungus or bacterium can carry on in the future.

There are two main types of reproduction. In sexual reproduction, a new **organism** is formed by the joining (**fertilization**) of a male and a female sex **cell** (such as an egg and sperm). In plants, during sexual reproduction, a male cell from a pollen grain joins with an egg cell in the ovary of a flower.

Asexual reproduction takes place without the formation of sex cells. Only one parent is needed. Asexual reproduction occurs mostly in **plants** and bacteria. It is rare in animals except in a few simple kinds. The offspring of asexual reproduction are identical to the parents and to each other. Sexual reproduction produces offspring that are different from each other and the parents.
See also **DNA, genes**.

resistance

Resistance is the property of some substances that reduces the flow of **electricity**. Resistance is measured in ohms.
See also **measure**.

respiration

Respiration is the process by which living things obtain **energy** from their **food**. During respiration, plants and animals take in **oxygen** from air or water. This oxygen joins with the food in a kind of controlled 'burning'. This takes place in cells all over the body. The energy produced is used by living things for movement, growth and reacting to the world around them.

rust

Rust is a red or brown substance. Rust forms on **iron** when it is exposed to moist air. It is a form of **corrosion**.

These are some objects that can be recycled.

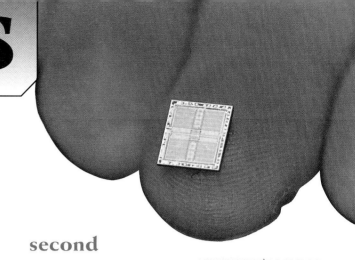

salt

Salt is a white substance. It is used for flavouring or preserving foods. The proper name for salt is common salt, or sodium chloride, which has the chemical **formula** NaCl. Small quantities of salt are needed to keep us healthy. Salt forms part of blood, sweat and tears. It gives sea water its taste.

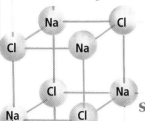

salts

In chemistry, salts are substances that form when **acids** react with **metals** or **alkalis**. Copper sulphate and calcium carbonate are examples of salts.

Saturn

See **planet**.

scale

A set of scales is a weighing machine.

A scale is also a set of marks, with numbers, rising from low numbers to high numbers. **See also balance, measure.**

science

Science is knowledge about the natural or physical world. Our knowledge of science has been collected and arranged by scientists. These are people who observe carefully, ask questions, make measurements and carry out **experiments**. Science tries to explain how non-living things and plants and animals work and behave. The thinker and mathematician Pythagoras (Greece, born about 582 BC) made some of the very first scientific experiments.

second

See **measure**.

sense

A sense is any of the ways by which humans or other **animals** can know about things around them.

Humans have five main senses: sight, hearing, smell, taste and touch.

The male emperor moth has the most powerful sense of smell. It can smell a female emperor moth about 11 kilometres away.

Some animals have unusual senses. Birds which migrate, for example, are believed to be sensitive to the Earth's magnetism. Some snakes are sensitive to the heat coming from the bodies of their victims.

To be sensitive is to be able to react to things. Eyes are sensitive to light. Skin is sensitive to touch, **heat** and pain. **Plants** are sensitive to **light** and grow towards it.

A silicon chip contains many electric circuits on it.

shadow

See **light**.

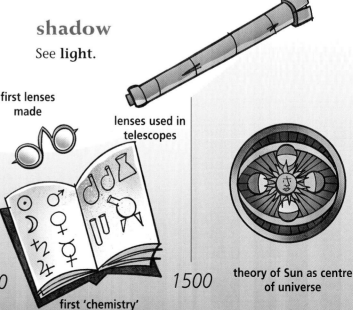

first lenses made

lenses used in telescopes

Observations and experiments have been performed by philosophers and scientists since approximately 500 BC.

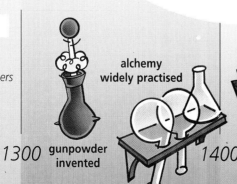

1300 gunpowder invented

alchemy widely practised

1400

first 'chemistry' books produced

1500

theory of Sun as centre of universe

silicon

Silicon is a grey **element**. It is found in many rocks, including flint, sand and **quartz**. Semi-precious stones such as amethyst and opal contain silicon. Silica, a **mineral** substance containing silicon, is used in making glass.

A silicon chip is a tiny **electronic** device. It is made of a small piece of silicon with many very small electric **circuits** on it.

silver

Silver is a precious shiny white **metal**. This soft metal can be beaten into shapes and highly polished. Silver is an **element** used to make jewellery, ornaments, some coins and tableware. Some other metals are coated with silver (silver plate). Silver is also used to make photographic film. Some silver is found in the pure state, particularly in Argentina and Mexico, but most silver is found combined with other substances as silver **ore**.

sink

To sink or be sunk is to go under or to make something go under water or soft mud. Something usually sinks because it is heavier than water.
See also **float**.

soap

Soap is a substance used with water for washing and cleaning things. Soap is made by heating **fats** or **oils** with a strong **alkali**. Palm oil and olive oil are often used to make soap.

soil

Soil is the collection of small loose particles in the top layer of the Earth's crust. Soil is formed when rocks are slowly broken down. The wind, rain, ice and other weather changes break down rocks and start to form soil. Plants grow among the rock particles and their roots help to bind the tiny pieces of rock together. When the plants die, they decay. They produce a dark, sticky substance called humus. The humus sticks the soil particles together and absorbs water. As the humus decays still further, it breaks down into mineral salts which are needed by plants.

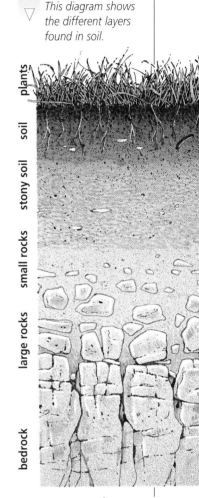

This diagram shows the different layers found in soil.

plants
soil
stony soil
small rocks
large rocks
bedrock

lightning proved to be electricity

gravity defined

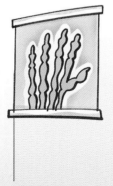

table of chemical elements proposed

1700

radioactivity discovered

structure of the atom discovered

1800

theories of relativity stated

structure of DNA discovered

1900

solar power

Solar power is the use of **energy** from the **Sun**. Most often the Sun's energy is trapped in solar panels. It is then used to heat water for use in a house. Solar cells can turn sunlight into **electricity**.
See also **power**.

Solar System

The Solar System is the name given to the **Sun**, and the objects that orbit it. These include the nine **planets** and their **moons**, and objects such as comets and meteors.
See also **astronomy, star**.

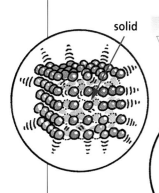

solid

All particles in a substance move, but they move more in a gas than a liquid and more in a liquid than a solid.

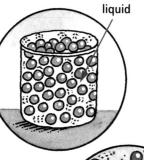

liquid

solid

A solid is any substance which keeps its shape and is not a **liquid** or a **gas**. A solid has a definite shape and volume.

Something which is not hollow and has no space inside, is also said to be solid.

gas

soluble

See **dissolve**.

solute

See **solution**.

solution

A solution is a **liquid** in which one or more substances are **dissolved**. The substance which dissolves in the liquid is called a solute. The liquid part of the solution is a solvent. The solvent we use most often is **water**. Alcohol is a solvent for some fatty substances that will not dissolve in water.

solvent

See **solution**.

A substance is visible in the test tube on the left but once dissolved it forms a blue solution as seen on the right.

Sound travels as waves. The loudness of sound depends on the depth of its waves. Quiet sounds have shallow waves, while loud sounds have deep waves.

sound

Sound is anything that can be heard. It is a type of vibration. Sound vibrations can travel through **air**, or **solids** and **liquids**. They will not travel through an empty space, or **vacuum**.

← quiet sounds

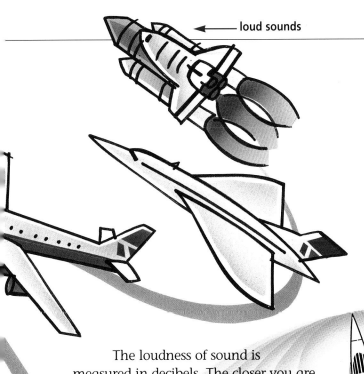

loud sounds

The loudness of sound is measured in decibels. The closer you are to a sound the louder it is. You can only just hear a sound of one decibel, such as a whisper. Normal speech has a level of about 40 decibels. A jet aircraft may reach 130 decibels.

In air, sound travels at a speed of about 330 metres every second (1190 kilometres per hour). Sound travels even faster through solids and through water than it does through air.

Many animals use special sounds to communicate with each other. These sounds are called the animal's voice. We humans make sounds with our voice box and our mouth. The voice box is in the throat. Inside the voice box are flaps called vocal cords. Vocal cords can vibrate when we force air over them.

We humans, like other animals, hear with our ears. When a sound is made, the number of vibrations every second is called the **frequency**. Frequency is measured in hertz (Hz). One hertz means one vibration every second. The highest note a human ear can hear has a frequency of about 20 000 vibrations every second (20 000 hertz). The lowest note the ear can hear has a frequency of about 20 vibrations every second (20 hertz).

Some other animals, such as dogs, bats, mice and whales, can hear high sounds which we cannot hear.

Sound is a type of **energy** and sound travels in **waves**. Sound waves can bounce off, or be reflected from, a hard surface. The sound is then heard again. This sound that is heard again is an **echo**. Echoes usually occur when a sound wave hits a large building or a cliff.

Noise is a loud sound. It is a sound we do not like or do not want. Noise is a form of **pollution**. The loudest noise in historic times was caused by a volcano. When the volcanic island Krakatoa erupted in 1883, the bang was heard clearly 5000 kilometres away.

sound barrier

The sound barrier is the resistance of the **air** to objects moving through it at the speed of sound. If an aircraft flies faster than the speed of sound it creates a loud explosive noise, called a sonic 'boom'. This is caused by a shock wave set off as the aircraft squashes the air in front of it.

space

Space is the whole area or seeming emptiness outside the Earth's **atmosphere** where the **stars** and **planets** are.

spark

A spark is a tiny electric flash. It is also a tiny glowing piece of something very hot.

When an aircraft breaks the sound barrier (that is, travels faster than the speed of sound), pressure builds up and this can be heard as a sonic boom.

species

A species is any one kind of **animal** or **plant**. Members of a species are all very similar, and adult males and females can breed with each other and produce young. Animals or plants of one species cannot usually breed with members of another species. There are about 1 million animal species in the world, and about 400 000 plant species.
See also **classification, kingdom.**

spectrum

See **light.**

speed

Speed is another word for quickness or swiftness. It is also the rate at which something moves. Units of speed include metres per second, kilometres per hour and miles per hour. Velocity is another name for speed.

spring

A spring is a piece of **metal** which can be stretched or compressed to store **energy**. Most springs are metal or wire coils or curved bars. A spring will return to its original shape or position when it is released.

Lightning is a huge spark of electricity between clouds or between clouds and the ground. The spark happens between a negative charge and a positive charge.

Stars are formed gradually by gases condensing on particles of dust which join together to form large masses.

Sun

star

A star is a huge glowing ball of **gas** in **space**. A star can be seen from the **Earth** as a bright, fixed point in the night sky. About 5780 stars can be seen without a telescope. There are millions more stars. Our Sun is a star. The brightest star seen from the Earth in the night sky is Sirius, sometimes called the Dog Star. Groups of stars seem to form patterns in the sky. These are called constellations.
See also **Universe.**

starch

See **carbohydrate.**

static electricity

Static electricity is an electric **charge** that builds up on the surface of materials that do not **conduct** electricity. It is caused by **friction** or rubbing. Static electricity does not flow steadily like an electric **current**. Lightning is a giant **spark** caused by static electricity.

steam

Steam is produced by **boiling** water. It is formed from invisible water vapour and can be seen when the molecules of water vapour cool and **condense** to form water droplets. Steam at high pressure drives turbines in power stations and steam engines.

positive charge at top of clouds
+ + + + +

negative charge at bottom of clouds
− − − − −

positive charge on the ground
+ + + + +

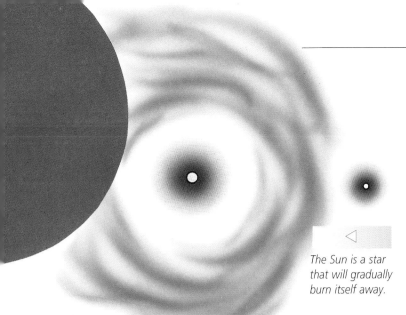

The Sun is a star that will gradually burn itself away.

steel

Steel is a tough, hard **metal**. It is made from **iron**, with traces of other metals and **carbon** added, and is therefore an **alloy**. It is used to manufacture cars, machinery, tools, girders and pipes.

Stainless steel does not easily **rust** or corrode. It is an alloy of steel and chromium.

sterilize

To sterilize something is to completely remove all **micro-organisms** from it by heating to a high temperature or by using chemicals.
See also **pasteurize**.

stratosphere

See **atmosphere**.

structure

A structure is something that has been built or put together. It is also the way that something is built or made.

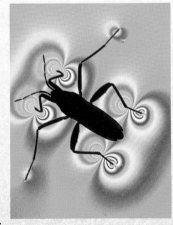

The surface tension of the water stops the pond skater falling through the surface.

substance

A substance is any kind of **matter**. A substance can be a **solid**, a **liquid** or a **gas**.

suction

Suction is drawing **air** out of a space. This makes a **vacuum**. The vacuum causes air or a liquid to be drawn in to fill the space. Vacuum cleaners work by suction.

sugar

See **carbohydrate**.

Sun

The Sun is a star. It is a giant ball of hot **gases** 150 million kilometres from the **Earth**. The outside of the Sun has a temperature of 6000 °C (degrees Celsius), the centre is even hotter with a temperature of 15 000 000 °C. The **heat** and **light** of the Sun are produced by a process called nuclear **fusion**. The Sun is a million times larger than the Earth, and without its light and heat, life on Earth could not exist. The Earth gets all its light and heat from the Sun.

surface tension

Surface tension is the way in which **liquids**, such as water, seem to be covered by a thin, curved, elastic 'skin' or film. Surface tension makes the liquid take up the smallest possible space. Some insects, such as pond skaters, are able to walk on the surface 'skin' of water.

synthetic

A **material** is synthetic if it is made by people and is not natural. Most synthetic rubber is made from chemicals obtained from oil.

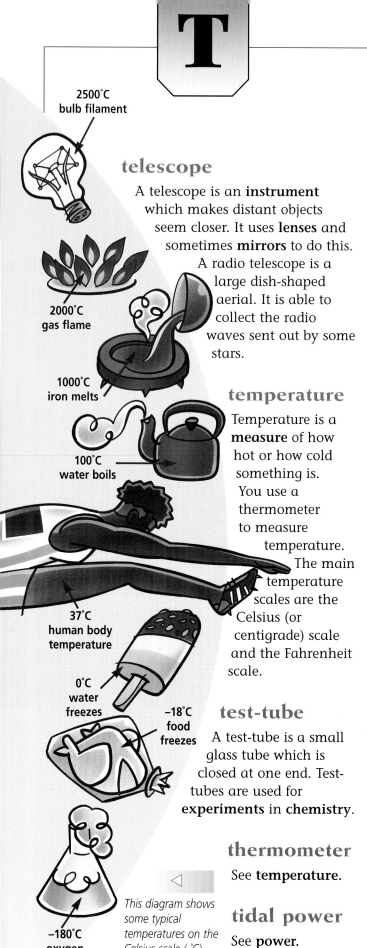

2500°C
bulb filament

2000°C
gas flame

1000°C
iron melts

100°C
water boils

37°C
human body
temperature

0°C
water
freezes

−18°C
food
freezes

−180°C
oxygen
becomes liquid

This diagram shows some typical temperatures on the Celsius scale (°C).

telescope

A telescope is an **instrument** which makes distant objects seem closer. It uses **lenses** and sometimes **mirrors** to do this. A radio telescope is a large dish-shaped aerial. It is able to collect the radio waves sent out by some stars.

temperature

Temperature is a **measure** of how hot or how cold something is. You use a thermometer to measure temperature. The main temperature scales are the Celsius (or centigrade) scale and the Fahrenheit scale.

test-tube

A test-tube is a small glass tube which is closed at one end. Test-tubes are used for **experiments** in **chemistry**.

thermometer

See **temperature**.

tidal power

See **power**.

time

Time is a period during which things happen. It is also a particular moment or period. Time is measured in years, months, weeks, days, hours, minutes and seconds.

You time something when you **measure** how long it takes. You note the time when something starts and finishes.

transformer

A transformer is a device which can increase or decrease the number of **volts** going through an electric **current**. Transformers at power stations increase the voltage of the electricity they have produced to a very high level. Then the **electricity** is sent across the country through cables carried by pylons. Near where the electricity is used, more transformers lower the number of volts again.

translucent

A translucent material allows **light** to shine through, but you cannot see through it clearly. Tissue paper and frosted glass are two translucent materials.

transparent

A transparent material is one that you can see through. It lets **light** pass through it so that a clear image can be seen on the other side. Clear glass and clean water are transparent materials.

troposphere

See **atmosphere**.

You cannot see objects clearly through a translucent material (bottom window panes), whereas you can see through a transparent material (top right window pane).

ultrasound

Ultrasound is **sound** of very high **frequency**. We humans cannot hear ultrasounds, but some animals, such as dogs, mice and bats, can.

ultraviolet

See **radiation**.

unit

A unit is a simple thing or a group of things that belong together.

A unit is also a quantity or amount used for weighing or measuring. A metre is a unit of length, a kilogram a unit of mass. See also **measure**.

Ultrasound can be used to see inside things. This is a baby (sucking its thumb) inside its mother.

universe

The universe is everything that exists. It is the whole of **space** including the **Sun**, the **Moon**, the **Earth**, and other **planets** and galaxies. Our galaxy is called the Milky Way and the **Solar System** is just a small part of it. There are other galaxies of **stars**, planets, dust and gases in the universe.

Uranus

See **planet**.

vacuum

A vacuum is a completely empty space. It is a space without **air** in it. **Sound** waves cannot pass through a vacuum, but **light** waves and radio waves can.

A vacuum flask uses a vacuum to keep drinks hot or cold. This is because heat cannot travel as well through a vacuum as through air.

The fan in a vacuum cleaner makes a partial vacuum inside the cleaner, so that air rushes in. As the air rushes in, it carries dust and dirt with it.

We also make a partial vacuum in our mouth to suck drink up a straw.

If air is removed from a can the space inside the can becomes nearly empty and a partial vacuum is formed. Then the air pressing on the outside of the can will crush it inwards.

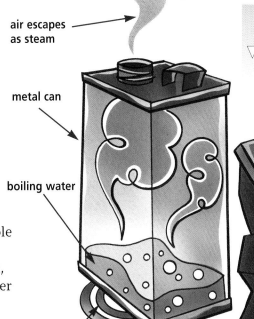

air escapes as steam

metal can

boiling water

heat

cap

cap replaced

empty space in can

no heat

valve

A valve is a device used to control the flow of **liquid** or **gas** along a pipe. A tap is a valve that controls the flow of water inside buildings.

A valve is also any device that allows liquids or air to flow one way only. A valve in a bicycle tyre lets air in, but not out.

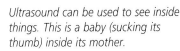

vapour

A vapour is **steam**, mist or some other gas-like substance. A vapour is formed when a **liquid** is heated.

Venus

See **planet**.

vertebrate

See **animal**.

Lava is red hot and becomes black as it cools.

vibrate

To vibrate is to move quickly to and fro or to make a quivering sound.

A vibration is a shaking movement or the action of moving quickly to and fro. The strings of a guitar vibrate when they are plucked. This makes the air inside the instrument vibrate, producing musical sounds.

The number of vibrations in a second is called the **frequency**.

virus

A virus is a tiny living thing smaller than a bacterium. A virus lives inside the **cells** of plants and animals. The virus forces the healthy cells to make more viruses. As a result, the cells burst and die. More cells are then invaded. Diseases such as flu, colds, measles, mumps and AIDS are caused by viruses. See also **bacteria**.

vitamin

A vitamin is one of the group of chemical substances found in the **food** of animals. Vitamins are needed in tiny amounts if the animals are to stay healthy. Vitamins are usually named after the letters of the alphabet. There are 13 major vitamins: A, C, D, E and K and eight different B vitamins.

volcano

A volcano is an opening in the **Earth**'s crust through which lava (molten rock) flows from time to time. Ash and hot gases are also forced out of the volcano. This is called a volcanic eruption. Eventually the volcano may form a hill or a mountain. Volcanoes can occur on land or on the ocean floor. A volcano may be active, dormant (resting or inactive) or extinct. There are more than 600 active volcanoes on Earth. The largest active volcano is Mauna Loa in Hawaii. It is 4168 metres high. One of its eruptions lasted for 18 months.

volt

The **force** of an electric **current** is measured in volts. See also **measure**.

volume

Volume is the amount of space filled by something. It is also the power of sound and how loud something is. See also **measure**.

70 per cent

74 per cent

Water forms a part of all living things.

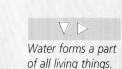

67 per cent

95 per cent

95 per cent

70 per cent

warm-blooded

A warm-blooded **animal** is one whose body stays at about the same **temperature** all the time. The temperature of the animal is usually higher than that of its surroundings – except in a few hot desert areas.

Unless we are ill, the temperature of the human body stays at about 37 degrees Celsius (°C) all the time. Most other mammals have a body temperature of 36 to 39°C. Birds and mammals are the only warm-blooded animals.

water

Water is the transparent, colourless **liquid** that is made of **hydrogen** and **oxygen**. Pure water has no taste or smell. It is neither acid nor alkaline but is **neutral**.

Water makes up a large part of the bodies of all living things. Without water there could be no life on Earth. Almost three-quarters of the Earth's surface is covered with water, while in the sky, huge clouds of water **vapour** bring rain to us. Water is the most common substance on the Earth's surface. It is also the only one to occur in three states, **solid** (ice), **liquid** (water) or a **gas** (water vapour), within the normal temperatures found on Earth. The average family of four uses about 3500 litres of water every week.

water power

See **power**.

water vapour

See **vapour, water**.

watt

A watt is a **measure** of **power**.
See also **electricity**.

wave

A wave is a moving ridge on the surface of water. Waves are most often seen on the surface of oceans, seas and large lakes. Waves are caused by the wind.

A wave is also one of the to-and-fro or up-and-down movements of **energy** or particles in which **light**, **heat** and **sound** travel. The distance between the top of one wave and the top of the next is called the wavelength.

wavelength

A wavelength is the distance between two similar places on a wave.
See also **wave**.

this distance is
the wavelength

△ Moving the end of a rope from side to side makes the rope move as a (transverse) wave.

side to side movement

▽ Moving a spring to and fro makes the spring move as a (longitudinal) wave.

to and fro
movement

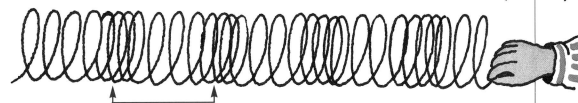

this distance is the wavelength

weight

A weight is a piece of metal of known heaviness, used on scales to weigh things. Weight is also the measured heaviness of something. It is the effect of **gravity** pulling on something. Weight is measured using a system of **units**, such as the gram and kilogram in the metric system. We weigh something to find out how heavy it is by using **scales** or a **balance**. Where there is little or no pull of gravity, people feel that they have little or no weight. Astronauts in space, where the pull of the Earth's **gravity** is weak, have no sensation of weight.

weight

parachute opens

air resistance

② weight

wind power

See **power**.

△ ▷

① As a skydiver leaves an aeroplane the pull of gravity makes her pick up speed and accelerate. ② The drag of the open parachute on the air supports her weight so she slows down. ③ When she lands, the ground supports her weight.

③ weight

support from ground

X-ray

An X-ray is an invisible form of **radiation**. X-rays can pass through many materials that stop ordinary **light** rays.

X-rays are also used to 'photograph' the inside of something, especially parts of the body. X-rays pass through the flesh of a body but not through the bones.

Doctors use X-ray pictures to show up broken bones, certain diseases and objects that have been swallowed. Dentists use X-rays to study decayed and growing teeth. X-rays can check machinery for cracks or faults. At airports X-rays are used to check luggage for bombs and weapons. Scientists use X-rays to study how **atoms** are arranged, while astronomers learn more about the **stars** by studying the X-rays that come from them.

△

This suitcase has been filled with bombs and weapons to see if the can be picked up by X-rays.

zinc

Zinc is a bluish-white, brittle **metal**. The main use of this **element** is to coat iron or steel to protect them from rusting. Coating iron or steel with a thin layer of zinc is called galvanizing.

Zinc forms many useful **alloys**, including brass and solder. It is also used in batteries and certain medicines and paints.

zoology

Zoology is the scientific study of **animals**. A zoologist is a scientist who specializes in studying animals.